A Time for Compassion

Spirituality for Today

Michael J Cunningham SDB

ISBN 0-9548388-1-5
© Don Bosco Publications 2005
Thornleigh House
Sharples Park
BOLTON BL1 6PQ
Email joan@salesians.org.uk
www.don-bosco-publications.co.uk

CONTENTS

Introduction

The Chinese have a saying: *May you live in interesting times.* This seems true of our era. Change has become the common feature of our culture. An old world is collapsing around us while a new one (postmodern) is yet to emerge. This affects every aspect of behaviour. Our culture is restless, distracted by the trivial and characterised by a loss of meaning and a deep cynicism. There are no heroes now. All have feet of clay. It may explain why politics seems to have lost its optimism and is dominated by phrases such as *the war on terror, the clash of civilisations* or *the end of history.* In this time of numbness as Walter Brueggemann calls it, religion appears, on the one hand to be in numerical decline, while on the other it is increasing in fundamentalism and simple certitudes: simplistic answers for a complex world.

But there is hope. A new interest in spirituality reminds us that we cannot bury questions of ultimate meaning. All religion has to undergo constant purification and renewal. When Jesus calls us to *repent* he is asking for a renewal of heart, soul and spirit. Authentic spirituality cannot shelter us from the problems of the world; in fact it leads us right into them, as is clear from the story of the chosen people in the Bible, who are led into wilderness and exile, to discover a God who does not threaten them or punish them, but calls them into a relationship of communion and intimacy.

This story reaches its fulfilment in the person of Jesus who moves us from a servant relationship to one of friendship, from fear to love: *Chapter 1.* He chooses a small group, chosen people, who will act as visual aids of what he is doing for the whole of humanity: bringing everything into union, everything in heaven and everything on earth. His mission is to bring all the polarities of life together, not so that one triumphs over the other, but in a creative tension, a new and richer unity is allowed to emerge. Even sin becomes the very heart of redemption and forgiveness. God invites us beyond a religion of the first half of life, one of law, observance and perfection, into a spirituality of surrender. The individual ego dies and we are re-born into a richer and fuller life of wisdom, forgiveness and compassion. This is the great transition into the second half of life: *Chapter 2.* Jesus reveals a totally inclusive God, who has no favourites but invites everyone to share the heavenly banquet. He reveals that, far from living in fear of God, we are in fact beloved of God, beloved sons and beloved daughters. This is the destiny of all people.

The Gospel strategy of Jesus is to create ever-widening circles of friendship: *Chapters 3, 4 and 5.* Friendship is God's great gift to us. Every human being needs particular people to offer warmth, acceptance and intimacy, so that our true self can emerge beyond the primal sense of shame and guilt, which is original sin. The love of friends gives us the confidence to move out to embrace *The Other*, the person, race or faith that is different from mine. Modern communications and technology have created a global village. Industrialisation has divided the world into rich and poor, but the rich world reacts with fear, not just to the cry of the poor, but especially to their presence in the form of refugees. Instead of bringing a healing vision, many of the world's religions seem to be increasing the divisions and the conflict. There is a need to move beyond limitations of *Our Story* to connect with *The Human Story.*

These circles of acceptance and forgiveness subvert and reverse our normal way of building a society with the rich at the top and the poor at the bottom. Jesus gives preferential treatment to the poor, in his teaching on the beatitudes: *Chapter 6.* In the *Great Gospel Reversal* the rejected ones become the teachers.

The way of transformation is what we used to call holiness. Such transformation leads us into the spirituality of compassion. The blending of the masculine and the feminine is one of the great life-giving challenges facing us in our culture today, *Chapter 7.* Much of the renewal of culture and the Church rests on the need to move from the patriarchal patterns that have dominated for so long. Men need to discover the sacred feminine and move from controlling, fixing and engineering change from without, to a more collaborative, compassionate style of authority and of living, one that brings about transformation and change from within. In the spiritual life, the patriarchal model of winners and losers makes no sense; grace is given unconditionally to all, beyond any concept of worthiness. Women need to bring their relational agenda and their voices into the masculine world of soul-making to embrace the need, not just for charity, but for social justice, as many are doing. The feminine voice needs to be heard in our Church and world. God has created us male and female and we need both for wholeness, but it is a wholeness that we all fear.

In the mystery of the Cross, Jesus goes further and reveals the great lie of history which is the creation and scapegoating of victims. He shows us how to deal with pain and evil, *Chapter 8.* Instead of projecting it onto others and blaming others, Jesus absorbs evil and violence, in the great theme of redemptive forgiveness. The lie of ignorant killing, which is the false story of history, is laid bare and uncovered. In complete vulnerability and woundedness, Jesus offers a new way of living in divine sonship, as beloved of God, which uses vulnerability and woundedness as the way into a new use of non-dominative power, the gift of the Holy Spirit.

The great transition to the second half of life is built on the death of the private ego. Life is not about me; I am about life. We discover that we do not go to God by getting it all right and perfect but through our imperfections. This leads us into the way of honesty and humility. The only sign Jesus gives us is not a set of answers like the catechism, but a path, which the Church calls the Paschal Mystery. This reveals the paradox at the heart of all reality, the opposites, which Jesus holds together on the Cross, as he hangs between heaven and earth, between the good and the bad thief. We are called to live this Paschal Mystery in our lives by holding the opposites together and allow ourselves to be transformed by them: human and divine, light and dark, good and evil, heaven and earth, original sin and original blessing, male and female, strengths and weaknesses, wheat and weeds.

Living a transformed life leads us to rejoice in the goodness and beauty of creation and of all people. At the same time it moves us to weep and mourn as we meet and experience the mystery of unjust suffering: *Chapter 9*. Such a life-style will not be perfect. Like the biblical characters, our journey will include some steps forward and some steps back. All of it however in the sure faith that God is the great re-cycler who can use and transform every aspect of our lives. As I learn to accept and own the darkness of my own wounds and shadow, I can move out to welcome *The Other,* the stranger, the one who far from threatening me contains the truth that I need. This has to be Good News, but it is not a pain-free path since we are, as Thomas Merton reminds us, *a body of broken bones.*

Michael J Cunningham SDB
Feast of St John Bosco
31st January 2005

Chapter 1

From Fear to Love

Have you ever been loved well by someone? So well that you feel confident that person will receive you and forgive your worst fault? That's the kind of security the soul receives from God.[1]

[1] Richard Rohr *Everything Belongs* (Crossroad Publishing NY 2003) p 105

We are living in a world threatened by fear. Despite all the advances in the technology of security, of increased searches at public buildings and airports, of better surveillance, our governments routinely tell us that a major terrorist attack on our cities and way of life is inevitable. We are told to look for suspect packages in public places, not to leave luggage unguarded. In a certain part of northern Europe, American citizens were warned recently to avoid public spaces and crowds. Sitting in Amsterdam airport a few months ago, I heard a CNN news story about the turning back of a United Airlines flight, from Sydney to San Francisco, because of a perceived terrorist attack. Very quickly I turned from casual listener to interested party, since I was booked on that very flight in the near future.

These threats are the new background and horizon of our lives. The politics of hope and optimism have been replaced by the politics of fear. Not just for those who travel. We are told that terrorist cells are already at work in western countries planning their next atrocity. At home the fear of violent crime always appears high on list of concerns in ordinary people's lives. We read every day of gun-crimes increasing. Even the young have invaded schools and shot dead their fellow students. While not wishing to exaggerate all this, there can be no doubt that fears, both personal and global, have increased in recent years. American psychologist Robert Sardello suggests that working with fear is the most central spiritual task of our time. [2]

Sardello argues that these fears affect the soul at a very deep level. They fragment our sense of who we are. I want to argue in this book that the question of identity, of who I am before God, is far more fundamental than the question *what should I do?* Unless we can struggle with and confront our fears, our lives will not have that fullness of joy and life that Jesus offers us. Our spiritual lives will appear flat and uninspiring. Crippled by fear, we will cease to be bearers of life, energy and creativity. It is interesting to note that one of the most frequently used phrases in the Bible is the greeting, *Fear not, don't be afraid.* It is used whenever God, or an angel as messenger of God, appears. It offers reassurance and comfort. We need to ask why it was thought necessary to begin God's messages in this way? The reason seems to be that in the history of religion most people have feared God rather than loved God. I think this is still true today. Religion, in other words, has more often seemed like bad news rather than good news. Why is this so?

Whenever God appeared in the Bible it seemed that someone or something had to be sacrificed, or someone had to be punished. It almost seems to be

[2] See Robert Sardello *Freeing the Soul From Fear* (Riverhead Books NY 1999)

part of our human hard wiring, that God is perceived as distant, a threat rather than a compassionate loving creator who seeks intimacy with human beings. In Genesis, Abraham is asked to sacrifice his own son, Isaac. We often read this story against the horizon of Jesus' sacrificial death. This reading not only distorts the meaning of what was really happening on Calvary, which I shall try to address in chapter eight, but it also deflects from the raw horror of what God seemed to be asking Abraham to do. In the event Abraham is stopped in the act of violent sacrifice, only to be offered an animal as a substitute offering. It seems that this story marks the moment in religious history when human sacrifice gave way to animal sacrifice.

Why does God appear to need these sacrifices? Looking at the history of religion it seems that human beings see God as someone to be feared, and therefore someone who needs to be placated on a regular basis by repeated sacrificial acts. Not much good news there! But if we read the Bible as a whole we find a very different picture and image of God. It is very much a developing understanding and is best characterised as *three steps forward and two steps back,* so you can find biblical passages of sublime intimacy, alongside others which seem to show a violent God. This pattern seems to reflect the difficulty we human beings have in accepting a non-violent God. So we project our love for violence onto God.

Although God has created each of us in his own image and likeness, many of the biblical passages reflect our need for a God whom we make in *our* image and likeness. The Judaeo-Christian scriptures don't hide this fact and are honest and direct in reporting the history of a people, chosen specially by God, but who frequently fail and get it wrong. In Psalm 106 we find a whole catalogue of Israel's failure to respond to God's love, expressed in the covenant relationship. This failure is described as a recurring theme in the history of Israel:

Both we and our ancestors have sinned; we have committed iniquity, have done wickedly. Our ancestors when they were in Egypt did not consider your wonderful works; they did not remember the abundance of your steadfast love. [3]

So if we view the Bible as a complete package we can uncover the development of religious consciousness and the gradual revelation of a God who, far from desiring sacrifices, is in fact looking for a relationship with his people. This relationship calls for the most amazing intimacy, reaching its fulfilment in Jesus. Jesus is revealed as the vulnerable name for God. In Jesus

[3] Psalm 106: 6–7

we see the face of a totally non-violent God. In Jesus, fear of God is replaced by love and intimacy. Throughout history most religion has focussed on winning a distant God's favour, by performing religious ritual, observing the correct formula, living morally upright lives and so on. The problem with this approach, and it is still very widespread, is that it puts the religious cart before the horse. In reality we don't have to win God's favour; in fact nothing we do can win God's favour. The reason is that it is already given. God's love is unconditional. It is a love far beyond any question of human worthiness. It is an experience of unmerited grace. This is the good news.

Paul Tillich once said that all of us needed to feel accepted at the deepest level of our being. To experience this level of love and acceptance is what we mean by salvation. Psychologists indicate that all of us need a *Significant Other.* That is why most people choose marriage which provides the stability and the security in which love can grow, in which mistakes can be made, in which forgiveness and healing can be exchanged; thereby allowing the love of both partners to grow and develop. The genius of the great monotheistic religions such as Christianity, Judaism and Islam is to move this need for acceptance to the transcendent level where God becomes the *Significant Other,* providing recognition and acceptance at the deepest level of our soul. The Hebrew Scriptures reveal that this God is not just providing acceptance for us but also seeks a relationship of intimacy and of union.

In reaction to the current stress on activity and achievement, on what might be called the outer journey of life, there are signs of a renewed interest in discovering the inner life:
In the postmodern world in which we find ourselves, many think that religion is in decline. External analysis looks at numbers who attend church regularly, on the decline in religious vocations, on recent scandals such as child abuse, the closing and amalgamating of parishes: there is plenty of negative evidence. At a much deeper level, however, our postmodern age is undergoing a crisis of meaning and there is a new search for a relational spirituality.

We humans cannot tolerate meaninglessness for very long. Something deep within us compels us to seek meaning and to 'invent' it when it is not readily available or when other forces militate against it (i.e. torture, sickness etc). The urge to meaning is primal (as in the infant's desire for the breast), prelogical, subconscious, fundamental to the very essence of human existence, just as it is central to the unfolding of cosmic evolution

itself. It is the over-riding governing force behind everything in being.[4]

Jung's famous claim that modern man is in search of his soul is beginning to be lived out in our postmodern times. Some argue that the search for spirituality is outstripping the religious search, and religion is in such a steep decline as to be heading for extinction. There are positives and negatives here, and having visited some New Age groups in California in recent years, I have seen the dangers of detaching spirituality from an institutional framework.

Religion is always in need of renewal and Vatican II embraced Luther's phrase *ecclesia semper reformanda.*[5] The Church needs to be re-vitalised and re-energised by the Holy Spirit. At present we are experiencing a shift from a Church which emphasised unchanging structures, was heavily hierarchical, non-collaborative, moralistic and defensive in the face of the world. We are coming to a new awareness of the spirit moving in the hearts and minds of all people, to a new sense of mystery at the heart of all reality, a mystery that connects and unites all things and all peoples. This new interest is happening against the background of fear and violence mentioned above. The danger is that the spirituality revival of our times easily becomes a marketable accessory, another consumer product to help us escape the harsher realities. There are many examples of this view of spirituality, as a life-style option, in our glossy Sunday supplements. It leads to a kind of *follow-your-bliss* spirituality and is modelled by celebrities who wear crucifixes and rosary beads as fashion items. Healthy and mature spirituality has to deal with the real. T S Elliot reminded us that human beings cannot bear too much reality. We don't so much need spirituality as a trendy life-style option, but spirituality for the long haul of building the kingdom.

But you can see where the hunger for a deeper and richer life is coming from. We are still emerging from a worldview, which has been described as overtly masculine. The period of the enlightenment has been largely mechanistic and rationalistic, placing all its emphasis on logical analysis and patriarchal control. In recent centuries religion has been more or less marginalised and reduced to private choice. This left the way clear for science and technology to dominate the world, and the resulting globalisation has widened the gap between rich and poor, while seriously threatening the ecology of the planet. The great myth of the enlightenment has been laid bare for all to see: the belief that being modern equals being reasonable, and that education and reason would bring an end to all conflict. The technological marvel of our instant

---

[4] Diarmuid O'Murchu *Reclaiming Spirituality* (Gill & Macmillan Ltd Dublin 1997) p 61
[5] The Church always in need of reforming

news-coverage on television reveals, not a world in harmony, but terrorists flying commercial airlines into skyscrapers in Manhattan, or killing innocent children on the first day of term in a Moscow school, or beheading westerners in barbaric fashion in Iraq.

Another myth of modernity or postmodernity, which is being revealed as inadequate, is the strong belief in the autonomous individual. The song *My Way* may well have summed up the twentieth century but we see today that no individual can carry the mystery and meaning of human existence. The postmodern invitation to choose my own life-style, fashion, values, including my spirituality, and to keep changing them to avoid boredom, is increasingly unable to deal with the complexity of these hard and threatening times. If my identity is built on the shifting sands of a constantly changing image, then it simply mirrors the Gospel image of the man who built his house on very shaky foundations.

The revival of spirituality needs to forge strong connections with the real world. This is not easy. Postmodernism has rejected all meta-narratives, all attempts at creating the bigger picture such as Fascism and Communism. These *isms* all claimed a kind of universal salvation through science and technology as the positivists had long proclaimed. There lies the clue. We Christians, with our spirituality of perfection, had almost lost sight of the basic flaw in our human experience, our human weakness, sinfulness and brokenness. In contrast to the myth of modernity, the biblical myth takes us into a very different landscape. It is the story and journey of a people who do not always get it right; they often get it wrong. Human reason alone can never fully understand the mystery of life in which we find ourselves; nor can we build the New Jerusalem by ourselves; nor can any individuals pull themselves up by their bootstraps to become perfect human beings. It is in this insight that a spirituality of compassion is born. As we learn to be gentle and compassionate with our own failings, we extend that gentleness and compassion to others, in their frailty.

Joseph Campbell once said that all religious myths and patterns of meaning are the same. There may be some truth in this but there is also a serious flaw. What the Judaeo-Christian scriptures reveal is a unique capacity for self-critical thinking. It emerges very strongly in the prophetic tradition in the Old Testament. It is equally clear in the constant references in the New Testament to the failure of the apostles and disciples to understand what Jesus is talking about and what he is doing. There seem to be two responses to the admission of failure and weakness. Either we are judged, or we meet mercy and compassion. The postmodern response is one of judgement, and a severe one at that. The tabloid press, and other commentators, are often merciless in the pursuit of their latest victim. People, in public and private life, are frequently hounded and destroyed by banner headlines, which spring from a venomous desire to blame and punish severely. Politicians, celebrities, Church leaders, criminals, asylum seekers, refugees are all tarred with the same brush. Of course there is plenty of human weakness in all of us to keep the new tabloid inquisition in business.

Our culture seems to have fallen into the grip of a very deep cynicism. Because our hopes for a better world have been dashed as we enter the twenty first century, commentators and journalists survive through destructive and often withering criticism. This kind of judgement also manifests itself in some contemporary humour, which holds humanity up to ridicule. There are no heroes and heroines any more. Everything and everyone must be de-constructed. Mocking laughter hides our deep cultural sense of being let down. Individuals are left to deal privately with their own sense of pain and disappointment. Since we are not able to carry this on our own, the natural tendency is to seek someone else to blame, and find recompense through financial compensation. This vicious circle of blame only increases the fear in our society. Parents no longer want to let their children play outside, teachers no longer want to run school outings, hospitals and doctors are frightened to treat patients in case they get sued for malpractice.

Healthy religion and healthy spirituality eventually come down to one question: how do I deal with my pain, with life's disappointments and limitations? This is where the biblical story reveals a very different response in the face of human frailty and weakness. We discover a God, for whom worthiness is not the issue; blame is not the issue. The God revealed by Jesus seems to have little interest in crime and punishment. This may surprise and disappoint many religious believers, who think that religion is about law and order, about doing it right, about the pursuit of worthiness. We see this at the start of the ministry of Jesus, when he is baptised by his cousin John in the Jordan. There is an attractive wildness about John, which underlines a part of masculine spirituality, which has often been lost in our sanitised version of religion. He works outside the temple and its sacrificial systems of worthiness, with its debt codes and purity codes, and pours water out in the desert as a symbol of the freely available gift of grace.

John hasn't got the whole picture; he still preaches a very judgmental God, and maybe that was needed at the time by way of preparation for what was to come. It is a bit like the recent film, *The Passion of the Christ,* which seems to glorify, by its obsessional treatment, the very violence portrayed against Jesus. It might shock some people back into some awareness of the life of Christ. The preaching of John the Baptist had that kind of shock effect. Jesus clearly admires John and says:

Truly I tell you, among those born of women no one has arisen greater than John the Baptist.

But then Jesus adds an amazing comparison:

Yet the least in the kingdom of heaven is greater than he. [6]

The significance of this remark by Jesus is often missed, but I think it goes to the very heart of the Gospel as Good News. As Jesus is being baptised the voice of the Father is heard from heaven:

This is my Son, the Beloved, with whom I am well pleased. [7]

Here we have a revelation of the intimate relationship between the Father and Jesus, a gift to be shared by all believers. This relationship ought to have the effect of transforming our lives. Often, however, in the history of the Church, we have been more concerned with the correctness of the ritual of baptism, rather than the experience of transformation. We take the good news and put it back into the old wineskins of correct moral behaviour and exact ritual observance. This is a starting point, but it is only for the first stage of life's journey. We all have to get started on the journey. We have to feel significant. We bask in the feeling of being special, of being sons and daughters of God. Unfortunately too much of our religion stays at the level of John the Baptist, of getting the correct behaviour right, of avoiding the punishment of a judgmental God. The Jews basked in the glory of being the chosen people; we Catholics have done something similar forgetting that our God is inclusive not exclusive. When Jesus left John at the Jordan he was led by the Spirit into the wilderness. His whole relationship with his loving Father was tested. In Mark's telling phrase, *He was with the wild beasts.* When he emerges from that kind of severe test, it is as if he says to John, *I like you and admire you, but I have met a different kind of God, not one of judgement but one of mercy and compassion.* He then begins his ministry of forgiveness, of healing and of reconciliation and he directs it to the poor, to the sinners and to the excluded ones.

---

[6] Matthew 11:11
[7] Matthew 3:17

From his prison John hears about this and he is not sure. There seems to be a hint of disappointment that Jesus is not breathing fire and brimstone. So John sends his disciples to ask:

'Are you the one who is to come, or are we to wait for another?' Jesus answered them, 'Go and tell John what you hear and see: the blind receive their sight, the lame walk, the lepers are cleansed, the deaf hear, the dead are raised, and the poor have good news brought to them.' [8]

Jesus is clearly *a second stage of life* man, who knows what to do with the winnowed chaff, the flotsam and jetsam of life that John doesn't have too much patience with. The one who understands the gift of the kingdom, the gift of grace and mercy, has moved to a different level. Jesus knows how people may be disappointed with him and the God he is revealing; that is why he asks us not to lose faith in him; not to let the beauty and wonder of the message fade. Many Christians seem to prefer a God who can be kept at a distance by performance related religion. Such a religion and spirituality keeps the ego in charge, as I measure my good deeds and practices. Jesus mixes with the poor and the sinners, not to judge and condemn them, but to proclaim forgiveness and acceptance, through the gift of abundant grace that can never be earned. It cannot be controlled; it can only be surrendered to.

Jesus seems uninterested in dividing the world into the just and unjust, the worthy and the unworthy, the perfect from the imperfect. One of the major Gospel themes is *The Great Reversal,* such as the last shall be first and the first shall be last. The God of Jesus doesn't seem to care about us doing it right; the heart of the good news is laid bare when we discover that we have to get it wrong, to really meet the God of Jesus. So the great Judaeo-Christian theme of self-criticism reaches its fulfilment in the recognition and ownership of our human weakness, and allowing ourselves to be transformed by it. We move from judgement through vulnerability to compassion and wisdom. This is the task of the second half of life, when we learn, through failure, that the ego has to die and we have to recognise our deepest need for God in poverty of spirit. This is the transformative journey of Jesus, which we call the Paschal Mystery. In the words of Richard Rohr:

We come to God not through our perfection (thank God!) as much as through our imperfection. Finally all must be forgiven and reconciled. Life does not have to be fixed, controlled or understood for me to be happy. Now, be honest, that is Good News! In fact, what else would be? [9]

---

[8] Matthew 11:3–5
[9] Richard Rohr *Hope Against Darkness* (St Anthony Messenger Press Ohio 2001) p 16

The God of the Bible is revealed as a God of great mercy. He is the great reconciler, or the great re-cycler. He uses everything in our lives. The most amazing fact is the way he uses our very sin and failure, as the place of deepest transformation. Jesus even points out that his Heavenly Father:

Makes his sun rise on the evil and on the good, and sends rain on the righteous and on the unrighteous. [10]

This gives us a very safe universe in which to live, it allows us to re-enchant the world that postmodernism has disenchanted. Instead of looking out at the world with eyes of fear that cut us off from others, we can learn to make connections and relationships, sustained by the confidence that the mystery of life points to a God who is loving and merciful and who has created each one of us in his own image. This is biblical faith; not an intellectual exercise in correct answers, but an invitation to undertake a journey of trust and surrender to the great mystery of love, a journey in which everything, mistakes included, can be used for our good.

Most of us hesitate to undertake this journey, because we fear the very thing that promises us life in all its fullness: a deep union with God. We are being asked today to embrace this earthly life with all its problems and dilemmas, not using religion to hide from them. A renewed inner journey into our hearts and souls will compel and inspire us to take part in the kind of world soul-making that casts out fear. This connects the private and the public, so that the inner journey of prayer and reflection leads to the outer journey of working for the poor and disadvantaged.

---

[10] Matthew 5:45

Chapter 2

The Great Transition

We are beginning to realise that we hunger for God and that for too long we have settled for far too little. The basic, primal hunger for God may be the least recognised and acknowledged aspect of today's highly publicised spiritual quest and our own personal journeys.[11]

[11] John Kirvan *God Hunger* (Sorin Books Notre Dame Ind 1999) p 12

What God seems to be doing in the Bible is creating a capacity for presence. He is not a remote God who is waiting to be placated by sacrifices, but one who desires a relationship of intimacy and union with every single human being. As with everything else in spirituality, it is always a question of *three steps forward and two steps back*. The journey of the Jewish people reflects our own journey. While we are attracted to God's invitation to intimacy, at the same time there is resistance and hesitancy. At times we prefer a God who keeps his distance. While God is finally revealed in Jesus, as completely non-violent and non-blaming, we still see plenty of biblical evidence of violence and harsh judgement in some descriptions of God. This really reflects the fact that blaming and judging others seems to be part of our human hard wiring.

Religion is often associated with special places where God seems more accessible. Anyone who has been on pilgrimages will support this view. Yet in the Bible we find a more challenging and radical understanding of spirituality. The Bible changes the focus from space to time. We are made aware that God is not in a distant heaven, nor is his presence restricted to special places, to holy shrines. What the Bible demonstrates, in a very radical way, is that God is totally accessible at all times, because he is present in his creation and more particularly in human beings, made in his own image and likeness. There is no doubt that to take part in a pilgrimage can be a profound spiritual experience. In a sense it physically re-enacts the daily journey each one of us is making towards God. The problem is that in seeking the special place and the special experience, we forget that God is found in the ordinary.

The story is told of a man who was having problems with his wife and family, and he did not get on with his neighbours. To escape all this hostility he decided to go on pilgrimage to a holy place. He left his village and, by nightfall, had reached the forest. Before he lay down to sleep he left his shoes pointing in the direction he wished to go so as not to be confused in the morning. During the night an angel appeared and turned his shoes back to face the direction he had come from. Next morning the man set off and came upon a village which seemed very familiar, yet somehow it was different. He seemed to recognise his neighbours, but they were friendly and smiling. Eventually he reached what looked like his home, and people who looked like his wife and family. They too were pleasant and friendly. Because his attitude and expectations had changed, he saw everything in a new light.

Once, while in New York City, I visited the Cloisters. They are situated on the upper east side of Manhattan, on a hill overlooking the Hudson River. The

Cloisters are a kind of re-creation of a European monastery, with chapels and medieval artefacts. I found myself wandering through one of the monastic-style gardens, surrounded by intricately carved patterns and figures. A touring group came by and one of the party asked the guide about some of the strange and grotesque carvings that bordered the garden. She pointed out that the ancient monks knew well, that despite leaving the imperfect world behind them, they could not leave behind their sinful selves. These gargoyles and grotesques were there to visually remind the monks of a very deep spiritual message. Evil is not over there, in someone else, or another group, or another nation; evil is also within me.

The spiritual life is a constant living within the tension of opposites, good and evil, light and dark, masculine and feminine, inner and outer, sin and grace, heaven and earth, wheat and weeds, strength and weakness. We will never overcome all these tensions, but if we hold them together they will begin to transform us. Our God is not just found in the pure and the special, in holy places like chapels and churches; our God is found in the real challenges of life, in the ordinary and in every day. In a sense we cannot transform ourselves, that is the work of grace, but by holding the opposites in tension we gradually become less judgmental of others, less willing to blame. Healthy spirituality is always a matter of *both/and,* rather than *either/or.* This is transformation, which describes what we used to call holiness.

By making time sacred, the Bible invites us to heal all the divisions between God and ourselves. God is fully present in our human experience, in our daily lives. The problem is our lack of awareness. That is why the question of identity is the primary foundational step in spirituality. Once I know who I am, beloved son/daughter of God, then I am in a safe universe and can open up to the fact that all human beings share in this mystery of identity. As we saw in the first chapter, a religion based on fear gets too concerned with getting behaviour right, with getting the words right, with getting the performance right. Authentic and mature spirituality leads us into the actual, into the real, into history, into relationships. The Bible reveals a truly incarnated spirituality, which led the Hebrew people on a journey that took them, both fully into the world with all its messiness, and also into confrontation with their own dark side. The chosen people are not just led to the Promised Land; they are dragged into exile. It is always *both/and.*

Eventually the Bible portrays God, neither as someone to fear, nor as someone with little interest in us, but fully incarnated in Jesus as the victim of human history. Many religious believers try to divorce the spiritual from the real. The God of the Bible is to be found in the real and in the flow of history. For too long we thought that we had to struggle to become spiritual, whereas the biblical revelation says that we are already spiritual beings, we are just not sufficiently aware of it, and the great religious task is to become fully human. The Bible is full of wars and adultery, double-dealing, betrayal, celebrations and feasts, of friendships and frailty. That perhaps explains while we Catholics did not like to read the Bible. It wasn't spiritual enough.

One of the problems that we have with the scriptures is that we hear it read in small extracts from Sunday to Sunday in the liturgy, and the priest is directed to preach on the readings of the day. This is a good way to get a comprehensive grasp of the Bible, but it makes it difficult to get a sense of its key themes. There is a discernible pattern in the ordering of the books which teaches a real and quite vital spiritual lesson. The early books of scripture, such as Deuteronomy, Leviticus, Numbers, begin with the Law. This is where we all have to begin. Parents and teachers are well aware of the need for rules and a sense of law and order. The young need a framework and boundaries within which to grow and develop. This helps us to get our necessary sense of identity and achievement. Religious development also needs this initial foundation of structure and security. What we soon learn however, is that none of us can keep the law fully and properly. We are not perfect human beings. This is a critical moment in spiritual development. It is the moment when we discover that ego-consciousness alone is not sufficient. Ego-consciousness cannot avoid suffering and limitation. None of us can reach perfection. Ego-consciousness is not generous enough or big enough to take us all the way home. There is a restlessness, a longing, that cannot be satisfied by mere human effort, however worthy. Only God can satisfy the human heart.

The Hebrew people were no different, as the Bible makes clear. It is the prophets who introduce the next stage of spiritual growth. These brave people demonstrate the kind of self-critical thinking that can honestly admit shortcomings and failure. It is not just individuals, but the whole people, who go through the failure of exile when all their dreams seem to be in pieces. They wonder where their God is in that experience of humiliation. It is only after that experience we reach the next stage, of the Wisdom Books, which hold the tension between the morality of the Law and the critical thinking of the Prophets. In the Wisdom Books we find the literature of compassion, mercy, serenity, humility and great trust.

This pattern is of immense significance in the spiritual journey. Recently I heard two contemporary spiritual writers and commentators, Richard Rohr and Ronald Rolheiser explain this in the context of two stages in life's journey. Most of us seem to get locked into the first half of life's agenda, where the issues are about control and observance of the law. The scriptures themselves make it clear that this is not sufficient. They allude to a second and more crucial stage in the spiritual journey. The author of the letter to the Hebrews clearly refers to the need to grow beyond the first stage of life. This letter seems to be written for people who suffer from what might be termed too much religion, in the sense of the performance principle. The problem is that this kind of religion puts the ego in the way and blocks God's gratuitous action. We need to get ourselves out of the way. Let God be God.

Eugene H Peterson underlines the point in a contemporary translation, in this passage from the letter to the Hebrews:

By this time you ought to be teachers yourselves, yet here I find you need someone to sit down with you and go over the basics on God again starting from square one – baby's milk, when you should have been on solid food long ago! Milk is for beginners, inexperienced in God's ways; solid food is for the mature who have some practice in telling right from wrong. [12]

Jesus himself was aware of this need to move beyond the first stage of growth, as he makes clear to Peter, after the Resurrection, when he contrasts his youthful years with the second half of life:

When you were younger, you used to fasten your own belt and to go wherever you wished. But when you grow old, you will stretch out your hands, and someone else will fasten a belt around you and take you where you do not wish to go. [13]

The reference to dressing yourself and going where you like, is Jesus' way of alluding to the first stage of life when you have to create your own image and identity, your own boundaries. Jesus then refers to another agenda in the second half of life. We see the same understanding in Paul speaking to the Galatians about the purpose of the Law:

Therefore the law was our disciplinarian until Christ came, so that we might be justified by faith. But now that faith has come, we are no longer subject to a disciplinarian, for in Christ Jesus you are all children of God through faith. [14]

[12] Hebrews 5: 12–14
[13] John 21:18
[14] Galatians 3:24–26

Paul is not dismissing the law since that is where we all have to begin, that is the first stage of life, but he points beyond it to a second stage characterised by grace. All we have to do with the gift of grace is embrace it in faith. Coming from a different perspective, Carl Jung says that the programme for life's morning cannot be the same as the programme for life's afternoon. In fact he says that what works in the morning becomes a hindrance in the afternoon.

So the first stage of life helps to build boundaries. The key issue in the first half of life is self-control. In the second half of life the issue is the giving up of control. It is about surrender. This is a much more challenging thing to do. That is why in many religions you commonly find people repeating the first part of life over and over again. This point is of crucial significance in the spiritual life. We need teachers and spiritual guides, who can help religious believers to make the transition from the first to the second stage. Healthy spirituality always leads us to transformation, change at a very deep level. It is the awareness of God's life, living within my deepest self. It is the discovery of what spiritual writers call the true self, the God-self.

The problem with the first half of life is that we think that we can do it ourselves. I can make myself holy, and good and acceptable to God, by following the Law as perfectly as possible; in other words I can transform myself. There is just too much *self* in all of this; the ego is still very much in control. The Law, in itself, cannot do this. The Law is a kind of container and the container is not the same as the contents. We have to step back and continually ask ourselves, *what is this mystery of life about, what is God leading us into?* Jesus himself uses this kind of language, when he speaks of the wine and the wineskins. They are not the same thing. We spend so much of our energy, as religious believers, protecting our wineskins. We continually promote *our* wineskins, saying that *our* wineskins are better than any other. We do not get to the wine, but life is all about enjoying the wine. When asked what the whole of religion, and sacraments and priesthood are all about, Richard Rohr answers, that it is to create souls that can receive the generosity of God.

This is not an easy thing for us to do. Instead of constructing an impenetrable shell we have to discover and accept our vulnerability. Daniel Dorr makes this point well:

It indicates that if we wish to live a fully Christian life we should not think in terms of mastery or independence, or rigid self-control. It suggests rather that a Christian spirituality is one which

is asking for support and a willingness to be hurt, to feel rejected and even betrayed. Vulnerability lies at the heart of any authentic spirituality. [15]

After all the effort and achievement of the first half of life, we discover that there has to be a lot of letting-go. All the things that we consider important in the first half of life are relativised by time, by the years as they unfold. We struggle to get qualifications, to get meaningful jobs, to be significant, to appear good-looking. Having lost its sense of the inner journey, our postmodern world places so much energy and money at the service of outer appearance and image. We try to build our reputation in the eyes of others. These things are not bad in themselves, but they are just too small and they put too much pressure on the autonomous self. This is the false self, which is very transient. In our individualistic postmodern world I have been taught to think that life centres on me; in fact life is not about me, I am about life.

Life can take any of these achievements from us at any time. I discover in marriage that there is no such thing as a perfect mate. My children may disappoint me in all sorts of ways. I may have to learn to deal with losing my job, or my reputation is unfairly attacked. The perfect holiday is never quite the perfect holiday. Age takes away our youthful appearance and energy. We never get it all together. We see injustices all around us; they never seem to go away. We all have to face the uncomfortable fact of the death of relatives, of friends, sometimes even young people. We may have to accompany others through a long degenerative illness. Eventually we too will die. As the Rolling Stones used to sing, *I can't get no satisfaction.*

All of this is a big defeat for the ego, but far from being a disaster, this is the gateway to the second stage of life. This is where the critical thinking of the prophets is applied to the books of the Torah, the Law. The crucial step here is to recognise my own dark side, my own part in the evil of the world. Evil is not over there. Too many, today, want to project evil onto someone else, or onto another race, another faith, or another country. Men project it onto women and women onto men. In families, fathers project their shadow onto their wives, and wives onto husbands; children project it onto parents, and parents onto children. Or we project it onto homosexuals or to asylum seekers, or to prisoners. And so it goes on.

The first half of life needs to teach us that we are special, that we are chosen, that we are significant. The danger, and we can see this in the Jewish chosen

[15] Daniel Dorr *Time for a Change* (Columba Press Dublin 2004) p 22

people, and us Catholics today, is that we then think it is all about us and everybody else is second best. We think God is for us and not for them. To some extent we Catholics had a way of recognising our dark side individually through the Sacrament of Reconciliation. However we were not taught to acknowledge it collectively, in the Church as an institution. Maybe this is why we are being humbled today, and asked to confront our dark side through the whole issue of sexual abuse.

We are being led today, as a Church, through the Paschal Mystery, the journey of darkness into light. We ought to have understood this, but we are no different from the apostles who tried to stop Jesus from going to Jerusalem and fled when he was arrested. Like the apostles, we have to be led into the mystery of paradox. For too long we Catholics reduced faith to a series of catechism answers. We had the truth; the others were dismissed as *non-Catholics.* That is why some Catholics today slip easily into condemning others, in supporting violence and war, as solutions to evil in our world. We thought we were the chosen people; we had it all and now we are being humbled.

I once preached a retreat to a group of religious men who had been hit very hard by adverse publicity regarding cases of sexual abuse. The Provincial had called a meeting in which they could talk openly and honestly about this crisis, and they did. Present at the meeting was a married couple who were clinical psychologists. Their advice was professional and to the point. What really struck me, however, was the spiritual awareness of this couple. As the men spoke of their pain and anger they were advised *to welcome their diminishment,* and not to seek to escape it too quickly. That is profound spiritual wisdom.

All religion eventually comes down to the question of *what do I do with my pain?* The postmodern world tells us to find someone else to carry the blame and try to get financial compensation. Religion has not been good at teaching us how to carry pain. I am conscious that I am being critical of my own Catholic faith, but I think this is true of all religion. In the Bible we see Jesus as God's answer to pain, but it is not an answer in the terms we normally expect. It doesn't solve the problem by taking it away. Paul tells us that Jesus absorbs our sin, our evil, our urge to violence, our need to punish, and thereby he reveals the lie of evil for what it is.

He doesn't fight evil; to fight evil is often to become evil. He takes its power away, by experiencing a violent death and coming through that experience no longer believing in the lie. The Risen Jesus offers no condemnation, only forgiveness. He takes away the illusion that the solution to evil and imperfection and failure, is to project it onto someone else. We hear this kind of rhetoric expressed almost every day by some political leaders, in relation to what is called *the war on terror.* It happens much closer to home, in our personal lives also. That is the lie of the first half of life and many religious people seem to be stuck at that level. We can easily baptise people by pouring water over them, but is the Church really leading people to conversion, to transformation, to making the transition to the second half of life?

Transformed people are easily recognisable. None of us is ever fully transformed; we are always on the way. Our lives are no different from the biblical pattern of *three steps forward and two steps back.* But the person in the second half of life has made the transition from judgement to compassion, from certainty to paradox, from cynicism to serenity, from disillusionment to wonder, from violence to non-violence, from excessive activity to prayer, and perhaps more than anything else, from fear to love. As lovers know, love leads ultimately to surrender and to nakedness.

Postmodernism has rightly called for deconstruction. The Hebrew prophets did that too; but they also pointed the way forward, not just by changing others but by facing the challenge of personal conversion. In some ways it is easy to unravel and destroy things. It is much more difficult to construct something new. Religious belief is often sidelined by the movers and shapers of our modern world. A renewed Church, with a renewed spirituality which is much more *both/and* rather than *either/or,* can lead us beyond the current agenda of decline.

Healthy spirituality can take us beyond the easy certainties of the first half of life, to learn to live with paradox and mystery. A spirituality that invites us to listen and learn, not just from our friends and neighbours who tend to reflect our own opinions and prejudices anyway, but to move into a wider circle of truth. In this way we can move beyond the necessary negatives of deconstruction, to a more positive agenda of reconstruction. At the heart of this reconstruction is an awakening to a God of immense compassion, who far from condemning our darkness and failure, accepts it, forgives it and uses it to transform us from within.

Chapter 3

Friendship as Gospel Strategy

I have called you friends, because I have made known to you everything that I have heard from my Father. [16]

Friendships that are real, friendships that engage the soul, are glimpses into the eternal love of God. When we really love someone else with a love that is total and a love that is true, then we know how God loves us. It is a breathtakingly unbearable discovery, isn't it? [17]

[16] John 15:15

[17] Joan Chittister *In a High Spiritual Season* (Triumph Books Missouri 1995) p 92

All religion and spirituality begins with experience. In time, dogmas, rituals, and ethics add a certain identifiable shape, and continuity to the original experience. One of the positive signs of our times is the attempt to get back to an experienced-based faith. We are currently emerging from a long period of what might be called dogmatic and ethical dominance. Dogma and ethics have their part to play in any mature religion, but if they are over emphasised, faith gets reduced to a series of affirmations made in the head; the spiritual life can easily deteriorate into performance based religion. Faith becomes certainty and our response to that faith is confined to moralism. Ritual is reduced to correct and perfect performance. It is a short leap from here to an image of a God to be feared, a God who does not like human beings. Today, as we are recovering a deeper understanding of the biblical journey of faith, in all its complexity and mystery, we need to see the importance of the shift from the experience of authority, to the authority of experience.

In this change of emphasis from authority to experience, Pat Collins identifies intimacy at the heart of the process:

If this shift is the interpretative key to the religious crisis of our times, the experience of intimacy is the interpretative key to most forms of religious experience. [18]

He uses the word *intimacy* in the sense of making known that which is innermost. Everything human grows through relationships. Relational spirituality is highlighting the need for intimacy; intimacy with ourselves, with others and, of course, with God. The whole of the Bible is a gradual unfolding of a God who seeks and desires intimacy with his creatures. The chosen people thought that their election set them apart as religiously superior to other nations. In reality they painfully came to realise that God had not chosen them because they were better than any other people. In fact the opposite was the case; they were quite insignificant in comparison with the great powers of the time. Carl Jung says that most conversions takes place not through words or ideas but through the power of images, which is why God chose these particular people. He chose to reveal his purpose not just for them, but for everyone. In the Acts of the Apostles we see Paul, the great outsider, teaching the other apostles how universal the good news really is.

While salvation is universal and for all, the lesson of the Incarnation is that human beings need to form friendships. Jesus is the great icon of God who came to preach reconciliation with all and for all; nevertheless he did it in a fully human way. His favourite description of himself is *The Human One,* which is

---

[18] Pat Collins *The Broken Image* (The Columba Press Dublin 2002) p 9

the best translation I can find of the phrase *Son of Man*. He constantly widens the circle to include all those who felt excluded. He reaches out to women, to children, to lepers, to tax collectors and sinners of all kinds, even to the occupying Roman power. He befriends them all.

Recent studies on the central doctrine of the Trinity have emphasised the relational quality at the heart of this mystery. Far from being remote and distant, the God of the Trinity is with us, for us and, indeed, in us. The biblical revelation reaches its climax in the invitation to share this very life of God. This is the whole purpose of our existence. Since human beings are created in the image of an inherently relational God, we are clearly not intended to become isolated individuals. Rather it is in and through our relationships with other persons, that we are who we are and become what we are called to be. In the Incarnate Word and through the indwelling Spirit we see what a person is called to be and Jesus sums up his whole ministry in calling his followers from a servant relationship to friendship.

We are all familiar with the picture of Jesus offering forgiveness and healing to all. What has received less attention in Christian spirituality has been the manner in which he gathered small groups around him, which were characterised, by a deeper level of relationship. These were his more intimate friends. He had a large group of disciples, co-workers and collaborators with whom he shared work and friendship. But in addition to that group he chose another inner circle of friends whom we call *The Twelve*. From time to time the Gospels tell us how he would withdraw them from the crowds, to eat with them to share with them and to pray with them. Here are just some examples from the Gospels.

From Mark:

Jesus departed with his disciples to the sea. [19]
The apostles gathered around Jesus, and told him all that they had done and taught. He said to them, 'Come away to a deserted place all by yourselves and rest a while.' [20]

From Luke:

On their return the apostles told Jesus all they had done. He took them with him and withdrew privately to a city called Bethsaida. [21]

From John:

After this he went down to Capernaum with his mother, his brothers, and his disciples; and they remained there a few days. [22]

---

[19] Mark 3:7
[20] Mark 6: 30–31
[21] Luke 9:10
[22] John 2:12

Jesus therefore no longer walked about openly among the Jews, but went from there to a town called Ephraim in the region near the wilderness; and he remained there with the disciples. [23]

Other passages could have been quoted but there is a clear pattern in all the Gospels. Jesus did not just send his disciples and apostles out to work; he frequently pulled them away from the crowds and shared moments of intimacy with them.

There is a further step. Within the group of disciples and apostles Jesus seemed to create a more intimate group of three, Peter, James and John. On several occasions he shared special moments with this intimate group. These ranged from the glory of Mount Tabor to his time of greatest suffering and fear in the garden:

They went to a place called Gethsemane; and he said to his disciples, 'Sit here while I pray.' He took with him Peter and James and John. [24]

The Gospels go even further in describing the human pattern of Jesus' friendship. According to the biblical scholar Raymond Brown there are two moments in John's Gospel when the Greek word *kolpos,* which means *bosom,* is used. The first occasion is in the prologue:

No one has ever seen God. It is the only Son, who is close to the Father's heart, who has made him known. [25]

This translation, like many others, uses the word *heart* for the Greek word *kolpos.* Jesus is described as close to the bosom/heart of the Father. The second time this intimate word is used is at the Last Supper on the night before Jesus died, when a disciple is described as reclining on the kolpos, the bosom of Jesus. This disciple is described without any embarrassment as the disciple Jesus loved.

We also discover in Jesus a remarkable freedom in his relationships with women. In the context of the patriarchal culture of the day this is truly radical and revolutionary. We find Jesus completely at ease in the company of women. The names of his close friends are listed in the Gospel accounts: Martha and Mary, Mary Magdalene, Joanna, Susanna and so on. He freely speaks to the woman alone at the well; he touches the hand of the young daughter of Jairus in a gesture that would have made him unclean in the eyes of the experts in the law; and he allows a woman, described in Luke's Gospel

---

[23] John 11:54
[24] Mark 14:32–33
[25] John 1:18

as a sinner, to touch him intimately by anointing his head, hands and feet, to kiss his feet, and to wipe them with her hair.

In these moments of intimacy and friendship we see Jesus revealing the love and friendship which is at the heart of the good news. Too often we Christians have tried to imitate the apostolic work and mission of Jesus while neglecting key aspects of his life-style. To this extent we can block the radical force and revolutionary message of the Incarnation. I have the utmost respect for all other faiths but our Christian faith is the most embodied of faiths. The transcendent God takes human form in Jesus and he saves us, not from beyond our experience by external act or decree, but by entering fully into human growth, risk, limitation and vulnerability. This has to be good news; every aspect of our lives can be open to transformation. Jesus becomes human so that we can become divine, not in bypassing our human experience but in living it to the full. What this teaches us is that we do not really know what it means to be human unless we know God. It follows from this that we can only know God through the experience of weakness and vulnerability.

The Jesus of the Incarnation is, in a sense, a disappointment to some religious people. Too often religion has wanted to worship an image of perfection. We can accept a transcendent God, but an intimate and incarnate God is almost too close to our human situation. Jesus radicalises the whole divine/human question when he says he will no longer call us servants but friends. This places our human ways of relating, our human ways of seeing, our human ways of hurting, and our human woundedness at the centre of our struggle. It asks us to move from the outside of life to its centre. This is the inner journey, which many shy away from as they launch themselves into yet another round of activism. A relational God is a very challenging God.

It is easy to be superficial. It doesn't demand much and the world today is attracted by style over substance. The whole media culture is based around a fascination with celebrities. While this may be harmless, it inevitably leads to a way of living vicariously through others. The explosion of all kinds of entertainment media has further underlined T S Eliot's comment that human beings cannot bear too much reality. We can easily engage in social activities, or politics, or sport, without any investment in our real selves. We do not let others get close to us. Part of the whole risk of friendship is the willingness to be open to rejection, or the pain of misunderstanding. Those who love us most have the power to hurt us most.

I can recall my early training in religious life when close friendships were seen as dangerous. The concern was the danger of sexual or lesbian relationships developing. While all this negative advice was being routinely offered across all the religious orders and congregations, I cannot recall anyone ever warning me about the dangers of not having close friends. There was always far more negative than positive advice. Here again we can detect fear rather than love of God.

The secular answer to human loneliness seems to invite casual sexual encounters. Society simply tells young people today to take precautions against an unwanted pregnancy or a sexually transmitted disease. The Church has not really helped secular society by its largely condemnatory stance to so many aspects of sexual morality, while offering little in the way of positive advice or example. Sexual intimacy alone is not helping to resolve the need for deep and healing friendships. The problem of sustaining any kind of commitment has deepened in the postmodern age in which so much has become disposable.

It seems to me that part of the answer is for the Church to take a much more wholesome and honest look at our wounded humanity, with all its limitations and weaknesses. This is the humanity that Jesus embraced and graced, by becoming fully human. Our redemption came from within the human condition, not from outside. Jesus took the risk of reaching out to others with the possibility, and reality, of rejection. He chose friends who were far from perfect. In fact the Gospels are very honest in their depiction of the failings of his friends. The apostles and disciples, with whom he shared so much, all deserted him in his hour of need with one notable exception. I think this pain of abandonment by his friends was just as acute as some of the physical suffering inflicted on him in his Passion. When friendships break down, the tendency is often to walk away. Jesus seems to take the opposite view. He takes the very man who denied him three times, and makes him the leader of his new band of followers. He takes the very failure of Peter and uses it, not to condemn him or attack him, but to transform him. It is here that Peter begins to understand something of the totally healing and forgiving nature of the friendship of Jesus. This is the point where Peter begins his transition to the second half of life.

Recently I visited an exhibition at the National Gallery in London of the paintings of El Greco. Three paintings of the figure of Peter fascinated me. The first, painted some time in 1580, depicts Peter as a penitent. It focuses on

Peter shortly after his betrayal of Jesus. His eyes are full of tears and deep regret. The second painting, completed around 1608, shows Peter with Paul, and marks that significant victory of Paul in opening up the faith to the Gentiles. In the painting, El Greco places Peter somewhat behind Paul. Here again Peter's face and demeanour demonstrate humility. A few years later El Greco portrays Peter looking up to heaven, almost in rapture. In his hands he holds the keys of the kingdom given to him by Jesus, but he is holding the keys loosely, almost apologetically. There is no pride and triumphalism here. What El Greco has given us, I think, is a picture of a transformed person. Peter is given power by Jesus because he has gone through failure and powerlessness. Once again we see the great reversal of the Gospel, the power of real transformation.

What has made this possible? Recall the scene in John's Gospel when Jesus meets his friends, the disciples. As on every other occasion there are no recriminations from Jesus. He doesn't seek to blame anyone for letting him down; he doesn't even mention it. He simply takes Peter aside, and rather than reminding him of his denials, he just asks him to declare his love and friendship. He reveals to Peter that all authority in the Church is first of all about love, before anything else. In the security of this healing friendship, Peter is invited to lead the Church with compassion, rather than judgement. He doesn't always get it right. None of us do. His mistakes lead him deeper into his need for God's healing touch. Ralph Waldo Emerson says that *there is a crack in everything that God has made*. If we are to befriend others, in a compassionate way, then we must first befriend ourselves, recognise our own weakness and brokenness.

The Gospels make it plain that, far from being perfect, the disciples and apostles often disagreed among themselves, argued, got jealous and often failed to understand the message of Jesus. A vital part of the mission of Jesus is the creation of a community characterised by disciple-friendship. Far from being perfect, the community would be an example to others of the compassion and forgiveness which leads to true and authentic *give and take:*

Our need for mutuality arises from our very flawedness and imperfection; it originates in the fact that by ourselves we are never enough. We need others to help us; we need others in order to help them. Thus, the question "Who am I?" carries within itself another, even more important question: "Where do I belong?" We find *self* – ourselves – only through the actual practice of locating ourselves within the community of our fellow human beings. [26]

[26] Ernest Kurtz & Katherine Ketcham *The Spirituality of Imperfection* (Bantam Books NY 1992) p 86

A community of disciples who are friends seems to be the strategy for evangelisation that Jesus chooses. Disciple friendship leads to mission friendship. The first level of evangelisation today has to be the ministry of befriending. It is the strategy for evangelisation, because human friendship creates the level of intimacy in which brokenness can be healed and growth happens. Such intimacy also mirrors, however imperfectly, the life of mutual giving and receiving we find in the mystery of the Trinity. Our recent cultural history, both secular and religious, sees the ideal life largely in terms of giving, but there are dangers here for the ego. It can be very satisfying to be giving to others. I am strong and the recipients of my charity and hard work are weak. It is perfectly possible to work for the poor and underprivileged and not be transformed.

Friendship moves the connection to a deeper level, where I am asked to reveal some of my woundedness. Those who live close to us pick up our shadow side very easily. Close friendship provides that deep level of acceptance that all of us need. Professional carers, such as doctors and teachers, need to keep a certain distance in order to do their work efficiently. Respecting professional boundaries is particularly important in these days, in view of recent scandals. But there will arise moments when a professional needs to move to a different level of true listening. Patients and students will quickly pick up whether they are being genuinely welcomed and listened to. If I, as an individual, have been listened to and accepted, then it is so much easier to do this for others.

Biblical spirituality cannot be lived in the head. It has to move to the level of heart and of soul. This is the pattern we see in the life of Jesus, as recorded by the Gospels. He healed people who were suffering before he began to teach them. Too much religion seems more concerned with teaching the right ideas and believing the right things. The Church seems to think that people are very simple and therefore need a lot of rules and regulations to prevent them from making mistakes. Jesus takes the opposite view. He regards people as being very complex, and so he reduces his message to a very simple one of creating friendship and community. He seems content that people make mistakes and, as we saw with Peter, uses them as moments for growth and transformation:

The real way to be biblical and to respect biblical authority is to do what biblical people did, and in the way that they did it. It is not to quote biblical sources or uncover the deep and secret meanings of biblical texts. The authority of words even inspired words, must

somehow be based in the de facto authority of accomplished deeds, redeemed peoples and living bodies. In other words it has to have worked somewhere, sometime, with someone, or it is an idealised abstraction. [27]

I think that this challenge is encapsulated for me in the whole issue of friendship and intimacy. All of us carry wounds within us. The usual and natural response is to build walls around our damaged hearts and souls. Then we throw ourselves into the world of work and activity and this can include charitable work on behalf of others. Those wounds then get projected unconsciously onto others. The strategy of Jesus is not so much to ask us to help or convert others; it is to challenge us to convert ourselves, or rather lay our hearts open to the transforming action of God. That is why he invited his followers to reach to those outside the familiar circle to an encounter with *The Other,* whether in the form of poor man, excluded woman, sick person, child, outsider and most amazingly of all, the enemy. Even the enemy can be befriended.

It is the person who is different from me who holds up to me what I do not want to recognise in myself. That is why Jesus moves us there. If I can welcome and befriend that part of me that is most broken, and of which I feel ashamed, then I am open to transformation. This kind of challenge is very difficult. That is why most religious believers resist it and stay within the pattern of the first half of life, of following rules and law, and feeling righteous about it. From this position of superiority I can then judge others as not being good enough. I can divide the world into winners and losers and I can sit safely with the *winners,* as I practise my religious duties with ever-greater accuracy and regularity. In contrast, the message of Jesus reverses all of that. The last shall be first he tells us, the Publican, who humbly recognised his mistakes, goes home more reconciled to God than the Pharisee, who has done it all right. The difference is a humble as opposed to a proud heart.

To help us to live the transformed life, Jesus calls us into communities of friendship, where we can receive affirmation, encouragement and forgiveness. This is exactly the pastoral strategy of Paul, as he travels the Greek and Roman world setting up very small communities, which were to act as visual aides for the Gospel he is preaching. As Paul went about proclaiming the good news he would point to these communities and say, *Look at them, there is something different there.*

---

[27] Richard Rohr *Near Occasions Of Grace* (Orbis Books New York 1993) p 47

In the history of Christian spirituality, and certainly in religious life, the ideal of friendship has not often been to the fore. There are many reasons for this and I would like to consider some of these in the next chapter.

Chapter 4

Friendship as Transformation

A friend is someone who is pleased to see you and has no immediate plans for your improvement. [28]

Would you allow your friend to have another friend, equally loved, equally important to your friend as you are? Or would that threaten your own sense of well-being, in which case, do you need friendship or self-esteem? [29]

[28] Anonymous

[29] Joan Chittister *In a High Spiritual Season* (Triumph Books Missouri 1995) p 91

Instead of a God of fear, who demands an endless round of sacrifices to win his favour, we discover, in the Bible, a God who invites us to intimacy and communion. We see the fulfilment of this in the person of Jesus who calls us friends rather than servants. Our God is fully relational and draws us into a relational spirituality, in which mission and community exist side by side. In spite of this, the history of Christian spirituality displays a reluctance to develop and promote the relational model. In these postmodern times it appears that the climate is changing, and a more human spirituality is coming to the fore. The culture itself is seeking a more relational basis for personal growth and a healthier world.

There is, however, still a long way to go. Many Christian believers, including priests and religious, still view religion primarily in terms of the performance principle; as a constant battle to win God's favour and grace. The problems are deep-seated, and Irish theologian Enda McDonagh, sets out some of the difficulties in trying to develop a spirituality that gives due weight to friendship:

Recent major dictionaries of theology, a minor growth industry, do not carry substantial or even separate articles on friendship. In the traditionally central theological disciplines of biblical studies and of fundamental and systematic theology, friendship scarcely rates a mention. In the newer disciplines of liturgical studies and ecumenical theology friendship is similarly absent. Only in moral theology, the theology of Christian living, in feminist theology or more accurately much of the theology by women theologians, and in spiritual theology does it feature. For moral theology, friendship is still peripheral although this may still be its most likely point of entry into mainstream theology, especially in the relational mode in which it is being developed by women. Spiritual theology is still unfortunately regarded by many professionals as marginal and derivative. [30]

McDonagh looks forward to the rediscovery of friendship as a major theological theme. It is strange that something so central to the lifestyle and mission of Jesus has been so marginalised in Christian reflection. It is equally strange when we reflect on the Hebrew Scriptures. The creation story, right at the beginning of the Bible, reveals a God who makes us in his own image and likeness. In a very real sense there is something of God in every human being. Unfortunately, we rarely reflect on the wonder and beauty of that message. It can't really get any better than that, and it reminds us once again that all we

[30] Enda McDonagh *Vulnerable to the Holy* (The Columba Press Dublin 2004) p 94

really have to do is keep reflecting on, and recalling, that ontological truth: we are all part of the family of God. This takes us back to the theme of identity and answers the question, *Who am I, at the deepest and most profound level?*

Ontology always comes before morality, being comes before doing, not the other way round. The fact that we are sons and daughters of God has nothing to do with anything I might achieve in the moral life. It is beyond human earning or achieving. It is pure gift. Spirituality is far more about receiving, rather than earning. This is a big defeat for the ego. All we have to do is to accept and believe this original blessing, which is far deeper and more foundational than original sin. Christian spirituality is nothing to do with placating an angry God who dislikes us; it is all about building on a foundational identity of goodness. We come from God, and the whole of the Bible is an attempt to get us back to that primal unitive experience.

Biblical spirituality is moving us, and calling us beyond separateness. In fact separateness is what the Bible calls sin. Most Christians see sin as bad behaviour; in fact the Bible describes sin as a state of alienation. It happens when we do not know who we are, or forget who we are. It is much deeper than individual actions, they are only symptoms. Sin is, in fact, falling out of union, forgetting who you are in God. Healthy spirituality is therefore about awareness, or attentiveness, not about performance.

This is a central problem in Christian living. Many people give up when they realise that they cannot perform properly, and yet all of us fail in different ways. So they opt out and give up, not realising that Christian living calls for a conversion, born in humility, and a surrendering of the ego, not correct performance and behaviour. Performance always comes afterwards, because morality follows ontology. What we do always flows from who we are: beloved of God. The scriptures both Hebrew and Christian are, therefore, describing attempts to get back to that original blessing and sense of our true worth and value rooted in the gift of our identity as sons and daughters of God. So instead of a God of fear and punishment we discover a relational God. God is constantly refining our consciousness by trying to liberate us at the deepest level of soul, to receive a God who calls us friends and offers us mercy, compassion, reconciliation and forgiveness. This is liberation theology working at the deepest level of the soul. God's desire and plan for all humanity is:

as a plan for the fullness of time, to unite all things in him, things in heaven and things on earth. [31]

[31] Ephesians 1:10 ESV

So the mission of Jesus is to bring to an end all separateness. All of us have been created to experience this unitive consciousness, this reconciling of all things. All the opposites will be brought together in Christ.

The story of creation in Genesis usually ends each day with the words, *and God saw that it was good.* There are two important exceptions to this. At the end of the first and seventh day, when dark is separated from light, and the above from the below, these are not described as good. This is important because these opposites and divisions describe our human situation. Our original blessing is, in fact, also a mixed blessing. All of us are full of contradictions. We are all familiar with the words *original sin* to describe this situation. I believe it is more powerful to use the phrase *original shame.* This shame describes our deep feeling of inadequacy, that no matter what we do, we never quite measure up; the fact is that we make mistakes and hurt others. Perhaps it is best described as a very deep feeling of unlovableness. I think for all of us it is experienced fundamentally as a sense of shame. At this point many people opt out of Christianity with its apparent endless reminders to us that we are sinners, that we are inadequate. Others remain Christians but tend to repeat the performance pattern of the first half of life. A more healthy response is to simply accept the fact with real humility. Again it is a defeat of the ego, but that has to happen if we are to be transformed into our true selves in God.

In creating us in his own image, God has imprinted deep within us a desire and passion for relationships, for communion. Since we are incomplete and inadequate we cannot exist as autonomous selves. We need others for completion, and this drive and passion is located in our human sexuality. So we have families and communities, and we need friends. We find a lot of emphasis on family and community in Christian writing, but not much on friendship. I think that the stress on charity, with its universal claim, has overshadowed the importance of friendship with its particular demands. We have been taught to love inclusively, not leaving anyone out and rightly so, but at the same time the human person needs the intimacy and closeness that only friends can supply. In the last chapter we saw how Jesus lived this way. Another reason why we have struggled with friendship is rooted in the whole issue of sexuality. We have to recognise that much of our teaching and advice in this area has been largely negative. The sense of unlovableness and shame, which is deep in all of us, is primarily experienced in our sexuality, in our bodies. It has rightly been suggested that the body has been carrying the human shadow of western culture for two thousand years. Unfortunately

Christianity, the most incarnational of faiths, has been a big contributor to this negativity. In recent years the sexual history of the west has swung rather violently from Victorian repression to unbridled licence. If we are to recover a truly Christian sense of friendship we need to go beyond the reduction of sexuality to genital experience, to include our healthy sense of sexuality as embodiment.

It is here that the problem of dualism has really damaged our spiritual health. The split between body and soul has done great damage. Daniel Dorr suggests that this begins very early in life:

> **Why is it that shame is so inextricably linked to what should be such a positive and enjoyable experience as sexual activity? It is mainly because from our very earliest years we have accumulated a whole reservoir of memories, of being shamed and being humiliated – and very many of these memories are about events which have to do with sex. [32]**

The situation often worsens in adolescence when a teenager has endless opportunities for shame and embarrassment, just when he or she is asking, Am I loveable or unlovable? The training that many priests and religious received in years of formation further reinforced the negatives. The ideal put before priests and religious was the workaholic or the perfectionist. Duty and sacrifice came first, and the model religious or priest had to be coolly detached and objective. In seminaries and religious houses the needs of the institution always came before the needs of the person. Physical personal space was often denied, and the needs of human intimacy were rarely addressed. Friendship was usually discouraged. It is not surprising that many of those convicted of abuse have revealed problems with intimacy. I recall Cardinal Basil Hume speaking to a group of British Provincials of religious orders, and challenging us to recover the gift of friendship and moving intimacy away from its narrow secular understanding of genital intimacy, into healthy sharing and interaction. This is crucial for anyone working in the area of ministry today. Preachers and teachers of the faith need some level of inner authority if they are to speak with conviction to our postmodern society. This inner authority is rooted in self-intimacy, intimacy with others, and of course, intimacy with God.

The recovery of friendship is a big task but there are some positive signs emerging. Both philosophy and theology are beginning to promote a more relational understanding of reality. Contemporary science, like quantum

[32] Daniel Dorr *Time for a Change* (The Columba Press Dublin 2004) p 100

physics, is revealing that everything is fundamentally connected. As more Christians re-discover the biblical message, we are moving from a God of fear to one who is passionately in love with us, for Jesus chose friendship as his way of relating to us. God is Trinity, God is relationship, and God is friendship. Instead of writing about the saints as if they were disembodied perfectionists, we are rediscovering their humanity and their friendships. In my own Salesian tradition we have the example of Frances de Sales and Jane Frances de Chantal, both saints, whose human love is expressed with genuine warmth and affection, and placed totally within their love for God. Today we are also rediscovering the mystics who made very real and very daring connections between human love and divine love.

Three words have traditionally been used to describe love: *eros, philia* and *agape*. *Eros* refers to desire-love and includes sexual love, *philia* to friendship-love, and *agape* to divine-love. *Eros* is the love of attraction and desire and it is initially centred on the desirer-lover, rather than the person loved. Attraction has to begin there and in a healthy relationship *eros* will grow to embrace *philia*-love with its emphasis on mutual respect and equality. The Christian ascetical tradition has generally been suspicious of *eros* but the importance of desire in love and friendship is being recovered today. [33]

Eros love, desire and passion remind us of the delight and pleasure that God takes in his creation, and God saw that it was good, and to say that we are made in God's image and likeness invites us to celebrate and honour that delight and joy. We can perhaps rightly criticise some of the sexual excesses and triviality of our culture, but perhaps we Christians, with our correct, cold and detached virtue, have not demonstrated our warmth and delight in life, in all its beauty and wonder. In stressing detachment, we forgot the other aspect of attachment, in a healthy *both/and* spirituality. This is powerfully symbolised in the traditional devotion to the Sacred Heart. The heart of Christ is out there in all its vulnerability; it is wounded by a spear. Jesus took this risk of friendship and was betrayed by Judas.

Healthy friendship provides an ideal space for *eros* to enhance and energise *philia,* so that reverence and equality are enriched by delight in each other's company. *Agape* is the word that describes God's gift of love to all. It allows us to love God and neighbour, in the way God loves. But *agape* love does not ignore human love. As McDonagh points out it must include both *eros* and *philia,* and transform them. Much damage has been done to many individuals by our not understanding this, a point McDonagh makes forcefully:

[33] Philip Sheldrake *Befriending our Desires* (Darton Longman and Todd 1994) writes from the Ignatian tradition. Eunan McDonnell *God Desires You* (The Columba Press Dublin 2001) presents the Salesian tradition.

In personal and ecclesial history *agape* as love of God has been used to suppress human relations with neighbour or spouse or children. The corruptions by which people are used as stepping-stones to God or ignored in the pursuit of loving God only, need the corrections of *philia* and *eros*. Human friendship and its delights belong in the broad sweep of *agape* as creation emerges from God and returns to God. [34]

St Francis de Sales also rejects the dualism that separates human love from divine love. We have one heart, he tells us, by which to love God and to love others. The more we love the more we receive from God who is love, giving us the capacity to love others. There is only one heart, there is only one love.

The renewed interest in the writings of the mystics is one of the most hopeful signs in spirituality today. These great lovers use the language of desire, of longing and of passion in their search for God, which is always uncovering God's longing and desire for union with every human being. Their language is intimate, poetic and extravagant. Meister Eckhart speaks of God being born continually in the soul. Julian of Norwich uses her favourite word *longing*. Pseudo-Dionysius defines God as *eros* or *longing*. The writings of John of the Cross echo the poetry of the Song of Songs.

Another way forward, being uncovered today, is a new understanding of truth. The western tradition understands truth as a mental concept. We are used to the idea of arguing and defeating opponents through the power of reason and clear ideas. The problem with that is, that it usually leaves the ego very much in control. It is the masculine ideal of truth and logic; it promotes judgement, competition and a dominative use of power. In contrast Jewish philosopher Emmanuel Levinas suggests truth is, *The Other*. This leads to a much more human and relational model of truth, which calls for a deeper form of listening. Instead of defeating my opponent in argument, I learn something of his or her unique truth, which is not a threat to my ego but enriches me in my own personhood.

In friendship I go even further. My friend is always *The Other* and someone I cannot possess or control. My friend is always a mystery to me, as I am to myself. But the warmth and affection of friendship allows me to share at a deeper level. Friendship pours fresh water over the dry and arid parts of my life, those areas of shame and unlovableness, which we all seek to hide. It takes time to reach such a level. For a married couple this is at the heart of

---

[34] Enda McDonagh *Vulnerable to the Holy* (The Columba Press Dublin 2004) p 104

their shared intimacy, and takes them beyond the initial infatuation to a much deeper place of love and healing. Their physical nakedness, in making love, becomes a sacramental symbol of this sharing at the level of heart and soul. It also allows them space for healing when the inevitable wounds and hurts of life's previous experiences come to the fore.

All of us, married, single or celibate, need some experience of this level of acceptance and healing. We need someone to laugh with and to cry with, someone to affirm us and someone to challenge us. In a relentlessly busy world we need some people to waste time with, and to celebrate the neglected joy and beauty of *being.* Beyond and within the general Christian call to love everyone, we need particular people, individual faces, physical eyes that can look at us, not with judgement and condemnation, but with immense love and forgiveness. We need hands that can touch us and heal the shame we feel in our bodies. We need arms that can hold us and tell us, despite all our faults and imperfections, we are loveable. Far from rejecting the body as inferior to the spirit, we need to recognise that our spirits and souls are embodied. We have always known this when we speak of the eyes as the window of the soul. I don't think we Christians have always understood why Jesus chose to become human.

Far from being something to be avoided and discouraged, friendship takes us deeper into the whole mystery of God's love for each one of us. When two people fall in love we often say in a joking fashion that *love is blind.* The good news is that God is blind to our sins. When Jesus appears to his disciples, after his Passion and Death, there is no accusation or recrimination. With Peter, as we have seen, he takes the very experience of his betrayal, and transforms it into an opportunity for him to declare his love. In a wonderful and physical image, he gives the apostles the power to forgive by breathing on them; his very breath is forgiveness. This image of Jesus breathing forgiveness into his disciples echoes the beginning of creation, when a divine wind, God's breath, brought the gift of life. When Jesus breathed his last on Calvary he asked his Father to forgive his murderers, because *they do not know what they are doing.* He is saying that his killers have forgotten that they are made in God's image; they have forgotten who they really are. It always goes back to identity.

This level of forgiveness is not easy for us as human beings. In friendship, however, we have a school of forgiveness. There is no guarantee here, and human friendships can break down beyond reconciliation. Nevertheless, a true friend is usually one who can accept and forgive the mistakes and stupidities that are always part of who we are. We would all prefer the judgement of a friend to the judgement of an enemy. Friends know something of our inner truth. This should give us great confidence when we think of the judgement of God, which used to be presented as a fearful thing. But, in judging us, God knows the truth of who we really are, our true identity. Those amazing words of Jesus on the Cross are a dramatic illustration of this.

In conclusion it seems that among the challenges that face us today we need to recover and integrate the three forms of love: *eros, philia* and *agape.* Such integration will help us recover a healthy way of relating in our postmodern culture. In this way we can offer a path through the excesses of our sexually obsessed secular vision on the one hand, and the cold and detached negatives of much of our current Christian output on the other. I think that friendship is the key to uniting the particular love of *eros,* with the general call to *agape,* the call to love everyone. Friendship includes both the intimacy and warmth of loving this special person, whose face, smile and eyes welcome me and accept me. At the same time friendship inspires me to go on widening the circle of love and compassion to all human beings. This gift of uniting eros and agape is beautifully illustrated on the two occasions in the Gospel that describe the tears of Jesus. He sheds tears at the death of Lazarus, his close friend, and he also shed tears for the whole city of Jerusalem which has rejected his love. The friendship love of Jesus includes both the particular love of eros and the general love of agape. Both can bring Jesus to tears.

In the final analysis, friendship also has its limits. No human being, however loveable, can reach into the deepest recesses of my soul. We are all mysteries even to ourselves. Only God, as the truly transcendent *Significant Other,* can touch us at the deepest level, where our *True Self,* our *God-Self* is revealed in all its glory. In doing this, God can put together the mass of contradictions that exist within all of us. These contradictions do not go away. We are always on the edge of tragedy, limitation and frustration in our poor humanity. This is a defeat for the ego, and it calls for a radical humility on our part. Many of us today find this very difficult. As the biblical story makes apparent, God seems to be looking for images, for human beings who will act as icons, who can carry at the same time the glory and the tragedy of human existence.

This is the essence of friendship. It is an icon of salvation, an image of transformation. Friends are icons of what God is doing for the whole of humanity. Far from being something to be avoided, friendship reveals the truth and beauty of humanity in a way nothing else can. It is a visual aid of God's reconciling, affirming and radical love. In uniting the particular and the general call to love, it leads to the transformation of our hearts and souls.

Chapter 5

Widening the Circle

We are already one. But we imagine that we are not. And what we have to recover is our original unity. What we have to be is what we are. [35]

[35] Thomas Merton *The Asian Journal of Thomas Merton* (ed Naomi Burton Bro Patrick Hart and James Laughlin New York New Directions 1973) p 308

As I was beginning a retreat for the Salesian Sisters in the USA, the news came through that Ronald Reagan, the former President, had died. Whatever way you assess Reagan's impact on twentieth century politics, one thing that made him a respected leader was his ability to see and articulate the bigger picture. That is a great quality in leadership. In the letter to the Ephesians, the author refers to the great plan of God, kept hidden throughout time, but now being made clear in Christ, as he brings *all* things together in unity, everything in heaven and everything on earth. Everything is in relationship. Everything is connected.

As part of this plan, God chooses images, people who will carry the mystery of what God is doing in every human life. However, election is not based on worthiness. Paul, the great outsider, makes this very clear in this more modern translation by Peterson:

So reach out and welcome one another to God's glory. Jesus did it now you do it!

Jesus, staying true to God's purposes, reached out in a special way to the Jewish insiders so that the old ancestral promises would come true for them. As a result, the non-Jewish outsiders have been able to experience mercy and to show appreciation to God. Just think of all the scriptures that will come true in what we do! For instance:

Then I'll join outsiders in a hymn-sing; I'll sing to your name!

And this one:

Outsiders and insiders rejoice together! [36]

The God of the Bible is clearly an inclusive not an exclusive God. The Jewish people struggled with this and so do we. We all enjoy the first part of the journey when we discover we are chosen and special; but we are less at ease with the second half of the journey, when we realise that so is everyone else. Given the fear-filled times in which we live, the need to move beyond fear of the stranger, of *The Other,* is crucial for the spiritual health and the future of our small planet. So in this chapter I want to try to discern what God is doing, not just in our own lives, but in the world at this time in history. This is the only time we have. It is a challenging time, a time of great change, but it is God's time. It is blessed and graced with the presence of the Holy Spirit in new and creative ways.

On the surface, our postmodern culture appears fragmented and lacking meaningful patterns. A deeper analysis reveals a search for connections, a

---

[36] Romans 15: 7–12

desire to build bridges of understanding, rather than engage in conflict. The climate of fear and suspicion, brought about by international terrorism, will either paralyse us or it will summon forth creative and life-giving energy, to bring hope to our darkened world. Technology, for good or ill, has brought us all together. As a force for good we can now communicate, by the internet and email, with ease across continents. Negatively we are all living today under the shadow of the conflict between terrorism and militarism fuelled by religious and political fundamentalism. While this conflict engages the attention of the world's media, the problems of sub-Saharan Africa remain largely unaddressed. The post 9/11 world is a more dangerous place, but it remains God's world. While evil seeks always to divide and to destroy, the Spirit of God is at work in our world calling us to a new unity beyond differences. This is the image of the kingdom of God. The appalling loss of life in the tsunami in South East Asia at the end of 2004, has uncovered a real sense of world-wide compassion among all peoples and faiths. Political leaders found themselves struggling to catch up with the generosity of so many ordinary people.

In the last two chapters I have tried to stress the need to see close friendship as an image of what God is trying to do in the world. As Christians, we need to stretch that friendship as widely as possible in the global village in which we live. Throughout history, the Church has struggled to respond to different challenges, thrown up by the culture at the time. We proclaim that Jesus is the perfect icon of God, yet we realise that our language and concepts can never fully grasp or plumb the depths of this mystery. In John's Gospel, Jesus himself tells his closest friends that their understanding of the mystery of who he is has to deepen and develop:

> **I still have many things to say to you, but you cannot bear them now. When the Spirit of truth comes, he will guide you into all the truth.** [37]

Although the word *catholic* means *universal,* many of us who carry that name have preferred a more narrow and parochial understanding. Our concern has been with matters within, rather than matters without. The temptation of Christianity is to be over concerned with internal Church matters and politics, rather than with the world, resulting in a trivialised Church, one that seems to have little relevance to the society it is supposed to transform. The Church should exist as a sign of what God is doing in the world. It is most alive and vibrant when it is not thinking about itself. Vatican II described the Church as *the Sacrament of the world's salvation,* which brings us back to the idea of the Church as an image of what God is doing for all humanity.

[37] John 16:12–13

Karl Rahner says that the Church has gone through two great crises. The first was when the early Christians, who had been brought up in the Jewish tradition, began to realise that the good news of the Gospel story was far too big to be contained within the Jewish story. The Acts of the Apostles describe the very real struggle and disagreement between Peter and Paul. The amazing part of that story is that it is the first Pope, Peter, who struggles to accept this bigger vision of how God is at work in the world, not just in the lives of the Jewish people. The Lord then has to speak to Peter in the form of a vision in the house of Cornelius, to convince him that this story is a lot bigger than he first thought.[38] This whole incident highlights the new and unpredictable ways in which God teaches us. Just consider how Jesus spent so much time, training and forming his apostles, and choosing Peter to lead them, and yet God uses a complete outsider, Paul, to widen and preach this vision of universal salvation. Our Church has long been dominated by left-brain, masculine thinking, which places a high premium on reason, logic and order. It is the control model that dominates all institutions. God seems happy to work outside our control systems. He uses outsiders, strangers; different people to reveal his truth.

According to Karl Rahner, the second great crisis of the Church is the move beyond a primarily European Church to a truly universal one. We don't need to be afraid of this, although many of us are. We have the Lord's assurance that the Church will never die. We do not have the Lord's assurance that the Church will never change. In the Church of my youth and upbringing in the 1950s, we had convinced ourselves that things would always be the same. How wrong we were! The years since Vatican II have been awash with change! How ironic that just as the Church of Vatican II began to embrace, rather than condemn, the modern world, the world itself was rapidly losing confidence in modernity. We find ourselves today struggling for a road map to navigate our way around the culture and the world of postmodernity.

None of us like to give up the spirituality of control. In many ways the corporate ego is more difficult to dislodge than the individual ego. This can be true of the Church, and it can be true of religious orders. We need visionary leadership. Above all we need collaborative leadership in the Church today. Deirdre Mullen, a Mercy sister who works at the United Nations, identifies the challenge facing religious leadership today:

This is a difficult time for many religious congregations. The glory days are over and we live in a different era. The era of globalization calls on religious to be fearless witnesses to the Gospel. Our

---

[38] Acts 10

witness must be ecumenical rather than sectional. We must be people who give an overriding loyalty to humanity as a whole in order to preserve the best in our individual societies. This calls for a worldwide community that lifts neighbourly concern beyond one's tribe, race, class and nation. [39]

In recent years the Vatican has published documents on, *The Laity* 1988, *The Priesthood* 1992 and on *Religious Life* 1996, all rooted in the theology of communion. This spirituality of communion is of immense significance in building a different kind of Church in a different kind of world, but it is not proving easy to move from theory to collaborative practice. It will be a Church that seeks to redress the imbalance between the masculine and the feminine. It will be a Church that really blesses and encourages a range of different kinds of ministry. It will take us beyond literal observance of law and duty and lead us into the foothills of contemplative prayer. It will be a Church that will really start to believe in the dream of Pentecost, which witnessed the great democratisation by the Holy Spirit. It will move from parochialism to a new universalism, from arrogance to a new humility. It will be a Church brave enough to lead us into the second half of life, rather than keep us trapped in the first part of life's journey.

Since the heady days of Vatican II with its high hopes of renewal, I think it is true that the Roman Church has tried to pull power back into the centre. I don't think we need to be too surprised by this. The whole story of God's people in the Bible is a continuous story of *three steps forward and two steps back.* This pattern is true in our own spiritual lives. So we shouldn't expect the history of the Church to be any different. Vatican II arrived a bit late in welcoming the positive aspects of modernity, just as the modern world was lurching into postmodernity. Modernity was itself a reaction to the wars and disputes, many of them religious, that had scarred Europe throughout the sixteenth and seventeenth centuries. Religion was at a low ebb, good and honest people sought to build a sane and tolerant world with reason and education at the centre. It was the inability of religion to handle changing times that led in part to the creation and growth of secularism, agnosticism and atheism. Religion was then marginalised, as science and technology became the new gods.

The secular world thought that religion had lost its force and energy. But men and women do not live by bread alone, or simply by the freedom to do whatever they want. Contemporary politics and economics have failed to deal

---

[39] Deirdre Mullen *Leadership: The Hard Questions* (The Furrow, The Furrow Trust, Ireland 2004) p 600

with questions of ultimate meaning and significance. Carl Jung underlined the failure of modernity when he said that modern man was in search of his soul. In Ken Wilbur's words, we live today *in the flatlands,* our lives lack depth and meaning, trapped in endless rounds of consumerism and the cult of celebrity. So many of our young people are caught up in this shallowness.

We have to take up the challenge of living a relational and compassionate spirituality in the real world in which we find ourselves. Sadly much of the religious revival which has survived modernity is rooted in fundamentalism, which is primarily a fear-based religion. It tends to deal with the pain and tragedy of human life by projecting it onto others. It clings to simple answers in a complex world. It usually has little tolerance for other views and opinions. In the past this may not have been so dangerous. But a technologically advanced world, such as ours, is also a technologically vulnerable one.

Our world of instant communications, through television, internet, email and text messaging, really has created the global village that Marshall McLuhan prophesied in the 1960s. We now see the world's pain laid out before us. Today we live in the conscious and visible presence of difference. On television and in our streets we meet cultures and ideas, which are different from our own. We see people who dress differently and worship differently. They follow different cultural traditions. This is often felt as a deep threat to our identity. The twentieth century grappled with questions of ideology, Christianity, Capitalism and Communism. The great challenge of the twenty-first century centres on identity. That is why religion has re-emerged as such a powerful presence on the world stage, because religion is one of the great answers to the question of identity. But here lies the great danger: religion, throughout history, has tended to divide rather than unite. The very process of creating an *Us* also creates a *Them.* As Rabbi Jonathon Sacks says:

In the very process of creating community within their borders, religions can create conflict across their borders. [40]

Sacks claims that the Enlightenment mistakenly thought that religion was a kind of sedative, as Marx famously said *the opium of the people.* In fact, it is fire. Fire warms, but it also burns and we are the guardians of the flame. The religious fundamentalism of our times has become a raging fire, which the culturally cool and detached West looks at with horror. Radical Islamists look upon the secular West as lacking any conviction.

---

[40] Jonathon Sacks *The Dignity of Difference* (Continuum Press London 2002) p 10

The Hebrew and Christian scriptures reveal a God who seeks to unite not to divide, to forgive not to condemn, to liberate not to enslave. As we have seen, this awareness of a non-violent and non-blaming God takes time to develop. The Bible also demonstrates how human beings still project their love of violence onto God. The development of consciousness which we see in the scriptures, with its *three steps forward and two steps back,* has its parallel in the life and understanding of the Church. As we struggle to read the signs of the times, we have to ask what aspect of the mystery of Christ is speaking to our situation today. In the history of the Church every age has had this task and some ages have done it better than others. The stakes are high:

We are called to show mercy to this generation, which feels so seriously threatened in its very humanity. We are facing a real ontological crisis, one that is experienced as such by people today. It is no longer simply a crisis of morals, or a crisis of atheism or agnosticism; what is at stake here is the human being as such. [41]

So the question is: *What image of God speaks to our world of today?* I would suggest it is the Cosmic Christ, the Christ who is beyond all cultures, European, American, Australian; beyond the white middle-class world. We have to be ready now for a bigger Christ who is asking bigger questions. This Cosmic Christ is seen as the liberator of the people, the lover of the poor, the God who is calling all history forward to a new sense of unity and communion. It is an understanding of Christ that sees the Church, not as an end in itself, but as a means towards the building of the kingdom. Jesus came to proclaim the kingdom, the coming of the reign of God.

All spirituality is participation in the Paschal Mystery. The Church too must pass through this mystery of death and new life if it is to follow the journey of Jesus. The great mystics tell us, in their wisdom, that we can never really know and understand God. They invite us beyond knowing into loving, which is always an ever-expanding mystery. So we can say, with some confidence, that the plan of God is to bring everything into union, to make us all one, to unite all differences, to bring about reconciliation and understanding between the races, between the religions, between different cultures and between the sexes. So the image of Christ for today is Christ the Great Reconciler, the Great Unifier, the One who brings everything together. But the *how* is of supreme importance. He does it not by force or coercion, but with patience and humility.

---

[41] Hervé Carrier *Evangelising the Culture of Modernity* (Orbis Books Maryknoll NY 1993) p 58

Too often in the past, we Catholics have stood aside from history and proclaimed our superiority. We have even coerced people into believing. What a travesty of the good news! We have told people that we are right and they are wrong. That doesn't heal any wounds, nor does it build any bridges. Rather than uniting people, and reconciling differences, we have, too often, divided them and widened the gaps. We need a new understanding of the Gospel of compassion, forgiveness and reconciliation. Pope John Paul II gave us two very powerful images of the Gospel of reconciliation. Firstly, when he gathered the religious leaders of all faiths at Assisi to pray for peace and reconciliation. Secondly, in Jerusalem, when he apologised to the Jewish people for Catholic sins of intolerance. The great spiritual journey of transformation leads us to a much humbler and less triumphalistic understanding of ourselves, both as Christians and as Church. In the bigger picture we are only a small part of God's plan for all of humanity. This is healthy religion.

All of us have a deep need to feel connected to something, to find meaning. In the past, healthy religion has made this connection for us: it told us that we are profoundly connected to something infinite. Recent western culture has for the first time broken this important link, what has been called the *Great Chain of Being,* or the *Cosmic Egg of Meaning.* People today have the huge burden of trying to give significance to their own lives, simply as individuals. Postmodernist culture denies any overall patterns of meaning. Each individual is left to create his or her own meaning through free choices. This places an enormous burden on the individual. That is why so many people today have very low self-esteem. I am left to create my own identity, through the endless choices presented by consumerism, or fashion, or the cult of celebrity.

Good religion suggests that there are three levels of meaning. Biblical religion, at its best, honours and integrates all three. The deconstructed society of postmodernism usually promotes only one level and thus over-exaggerates it. The three levels are:

Most people today get trapped in the smallest story and secular individualists and liberals operate here; it is all about *my* choices, *my* freedom. In contrast, conservatives tend to get trapped at the second level: *our country, flag* etc., and the fundamentalists distort the third level. The saint or the transformed person can inhabit all three.

MY STORY

This is the language of modern psychology. Our parents, certainly our grand-parents, probably never had this. Traditional religious life paid little attention to this personal story. All of us need to create healthy boundaries, but we cannot remain there. Women are often better at articulating these feelings than men. Here are some of the issues that I feel about, such as what makes me feel inferior, superior, right, wrong, handicapped or gifted. This is all the postmodern person has: my feelings, my pain, my prestige, my possessions, my image, my reputation. The realm of the small self is just not big enough to carry meaning on its own. The stage is too big for us to live as autonomous isolated individuals. If people get trapped here they are usually very quick to blame and project pain onto others, and we see so much of this in our culture today.

OUR STORY

This is a larger frame of meaning. It includes *our* group, *our* community, *our* parish, *our* religious order, *our* religion, *our* team, *our* nationality, *our* ethnic group. We are essentially social beings and we need this extra level of meaning and relationships. Here men are more comfortable with the values of group loyalty. This is the world of symbols and flags, patriotism, *my country right or wrong.* It taps into loyalty, and most wars are usually fought at this level. It often needs a group enemy, on whom we can project all our evils and problems. It promotes the ideal of dying for a cause. Much Christianity functions at this level of cultural loyalty and identity. Catholics felt it very strongly before Vatican II, with all the nostalgia for Latin, fasting on Fridays, even religious habits. We see this perpetuated in Muslim women today. A lot of this is positive in terms of relational values, family, country etc., but once you move into the real centre and discover who you are in God, you will need this second level less and less.

Here we discover the great patterns of meaning that all religions point to. This is true transcendence and it holds the other two levels together and rescues them from turning in on themselves. This is the realm of the Spirit and the True Self, the Larger Self, the God Self. It embraces everything and rejects nothing. Here everything belongs. Postmodernism has rejected this level of meaning, and we are suffering the consequences of living without this larger canopy of meaning that gives true significance to our lives.

Biblical religion honours all three levels, and, at its best, calls for integration. All three great monotheistic religions ultimately reveal this to be a personal God. This level frees us from being trapped in the tyranny of just My Story, *I Am,* and the idolatry of Our Story, *We Are.* But it respects the importance of both my personal story and the community story. If you try to go straight to Spirit, without the personal and the communal story, you end up in fundamentalism. It looks like passionate religion, but it lacks biblical wisdom and love. It produces hatred and intolerance. Saul of Tarsus was like that until he met Jesus. All three levels are honoured in the realm of the mystic, the prophet, the saint, the whole man or woman.

It leads beyond small group loyalty, beyond the calculative mind, that seeks winners and losers, good guys and bad guys. This is the contemplative mind. It deals with the dark side of life, not by rejection, or denial, or projection onto *The Other* (person, group, nation or faith), but owning it, acknowledging it, and allowing it, is to be forgiven and transformed.

All great religion ultimately forces us to confront pain, either in our personal lives or in our world. This is the core spiritual question. Either we project our pain onto someone else, or we allow it to transform us. The wounds then become sacred. Instead of killing the stranger, or ignoring him, or despising him, I can learn his story both personal and communal. Then I am learning to trust, to embrace, to learn from, and to love the human story which God is writing and blessing in every human being. It cannot happen without pain. This is underlined in a memorable phrase by Thomas Merton:

> **As long as we are on earth, the love that unites us will bring us suffering by our very contact with one another, because this love is the resetting of a Body of broken bones. Even saints cannot live on this earth without some anguish, without some pain at the differences that come between them.** [42]

---

[42] Thomas Merton *New Seeds of Contemplation* (New Directions NY 1972) p 72

This is to understand biblical truth as *The Other,* as Levinas makes clear. When I know who I am in God, I have the freedom to allow *The Other* to change me. It can't happen without the painful resetting of our broken bones.

I began by speaking of the fear and mistrust at the heart of our world today. We need to counter this fear by recognising the energy and love of the Holy Spirit expressed in difference and in variety. When we can honour and respect differences we can then discover the fundamental unity in all human beings who reflect the image of God in all its richness and endless variety. This is expressed powerfully in those words of Jesus: *I was a stranger and you made me welcome.*

Chapter 6

The Path to Transformation

God dwells within us. He is no longer a shining presence in the heavens, but a humble presence in the mud of our inner being. [43]

[43] Jean Vanier *Our Journey Home* (Hodder & Stoughton 1997) p 250

The biblical God is revealed as creating a capacity for presence, for union. Despite our doubts about worthiness, often felt as a kind of primal shame, God is presented as the one who clothes our nakedness in the way he sewed clothes for the sinful Adam and Eve. He wants to clothe our vulnerability and invite us back to a life of relationship, a life of love, a life of presence. Too often we mistakenly reduce this life to dutiful performance and religious practice. Sadly this usually leaves the ego in charge. What Jesus invites us to do is to embark on a much more risky journey, not into the realms of successful material achievement, but into a series of encounters with the poor and the vulnerable. Not in order that we, in our strength and in our charity, can reach out to the lowly poor; but that the opposite will take place. The only purpose of working for the poor and vulnerable is to realise that I am poor and vulnerable.

This is transformation. I cannot make it happen; it is not subject to achievement and effort; it has to be waited on in powerlessness and meekness. It is the gift of God, who chooses to identify with the poor and the vulnerable to such an extent, that what is done to the least of the brothers and sisters is done to God himself. Jesus draws us into this space and calls it blessed. Here again we see the great reversal of the Gospel. Here the neighbour is transformed from threat to life-giver. Christians are not exhorted to be charitable in order to feel good. Engagement with *The Other* is the place where the Paschal Mystery will begin to change from an idea in the head, or even in the liturgy, to a place of death and new life. The journey of the second half of life cannot begin without a death, without the shedding of blood. What has to die is the private self, the private ego, the autonomous self. Then we are blessed in the biblical sense by One who is greater than we are, who gives us a new identity bigger than the private self:

> **One could say that the central theme of the biblical revelation is to call people to encounters with otherness; the alien, the sinner, the Samaritan, the Gentile, the hidden and denied self, angels unaware. And all of these perhaps, in preparation and training for hopeful meetings with true transcendence, the Absolute Other. We need practice in moving outside our comfort zones. It is never a natural response. [44]**

The recovery of friendship, in Christian spirituality, will help to restore desire, passion and longing into other aspects of our lives. If, as Francis de Sales reminds us, we have one heart by which to love God and others, then when that love is touched and enlivened then our hearts will widen to feel passion

---

[44] Richard Rohr *Job and the Mystery of Suffering* (Gracewing Herefordshire 1996) p 157

for the world. This passion becomes compassion, as we stand alongside those who suffer in whatever form.

Jesus tells us that nobody should put new wine into old wineskins, so he spends his public ministry trying to describe this new reality of grace and compassion. The favourite metaphor in the synoptics is the *kingdom of God.* John's Gospel speaks of *eternal life.* Paul will later speak about *the new creation* and *living in Christ.* The kingdom is the new reality; it is a mystery that Jesus describes in parables. It is always now, but not yet, present now, but not fully. We cannot possess the kingdom; the kingdom possesses us.

Immediately after his baptism, we are told that Jesus was led by the Spirit into the wilderness. Matthew makes it very clear that he was led there to be tempted by the devil. Mark tells us that he was with the wild beasts. What happens here is fascinating because Satan is desperate to break this loving relationship between Jesus and his Father. All his temptations are aimed at the humanity of Jesus; *don't accept human poverty and limitations.* It is as if the devil doesn't mind Jesus being God; what he doesn't want is a God who is fully human. It has often been remarked how Christian spirituality has often tried to make us into angels, and forgotten our humanity. We have never been really at home with an incarnational God, a God that we can know and love in the flesh. This period in the wilderness shows Jesus teaching us not to be afraid of the inner journey, not to be afraid of loneliness and of powerlessness, because it is the way to transformation.

When Jesus emerges from the wilderness to begin his ministry he reveals a different God from that of John the Baptist. As we mentioned in Chapter One, John fitted the mould of a rather angry prophet; his lifestyle was sparse and ascetic. Jesus is different. He admires and praises John, but his time in the wilderness has rooted him in the experience and conviction that he has a loving and compassionate Father. He has met a different God, a God who invites all of us into a relationship of love and intimacy. With Jesus something entirely new has appeared in humanity's relationship with God, so while Jesus praises John, he describes the least in the kingdom as even greater than him.

His whole ministry is centred on trying to get people to change, to be converted, so as to be able to accept and live in this relationship of grace and mercy. But he does it in a different way. Where John denounces sinners and calls them to repentance, Jesus meets them, talks with them and, in an extraordinary gesture, he dines with them. The Gospel symbol of the banquet, to which all are invited, is one of the more powerful and radical signs used by Jesus as a kind of visual aid of the gift of grace, of the presence of the kingdom, of something new breaking into history. Walter Brueggemann underlines the truly radical nature of the compassion and mercy of Jesus, symbolised in the act of eating with outcasts:

The outcasts were the product of a legal arrangement that determined what was acceptable and unacceptable, clean and unclean, right and wrong. Crossing over the barrier of right and wrong implied that in the dispensing of mercy the wrong were as entitled as the right, and therefore all meaningful distinctions were obliterated. [45]

As a way of leading his followers into this ethos of mercy and compassion, Jesus offers the eight beatitudes. In this teaching we see God reversing the normal way of looking at history. Every culture looks at history from the top; Jesus looks at history from the bottom. Many of the great biblical figures, such as Moses, longed to see the face of God. Jesus now reveals the face of God in suffering humanity. The loving Father, who calls Jesus his beloved son, also looks on suffering humanity and sees his reflection in it. Jesus teaches his disciples to see the beauty of God in each other, through the gift of friendship. In the beatitudes, he opens up the mystery of suffering and reveals the pain of God in the faces of the poor and excluded ones. In beauty and suffering, the Paschal Mystery becomes real and transformative. This is a path, not an answer; it is the paschal journey, sometimes light and sometimes dark. Human life is sometimes tragic and sometimes pleasant; but Jesus tells us that it is always blessed.

There are many who work for the poor, for the disadvantaged, for young people in need, but they are not transformed people. Look at all the great revolutions of history, which usually begin on the left of the political spectrum to root out injustice, and end up on the right: e.g. the Russian, French, American revolutions. Social transformation without personal transformation simply replaces one set of egos with another. Transformation happens when we can allow ourselves to hold the tensions of the great paradoxes of life, when we can hold opposites together. We have to stop trusting in our egos and start trusting in God. Not in a God who makes everything wonderful and pain-free, but in a God who loves me and yet invites me into poverty, a God who loves me and yet asks me to deal with the death of loved ones, or the death of young people I have taught, or a sickness I don't want. It is far from easy to love a God who asks me to rejoice when my name and reputation are being destroyed. If I can come through these experiences, without becoming

[45] Walter Brueggemann *The Prophetic Imagination* (Fortress Press Minneapolis 2001) p 85

bitter or angry, then I am open to transformation. These experiences reveal to me the unexpected face of God; not a God of triumph and glory, but a God who is revealed as vulnerable and even powerless, because ultimately he is a God of compassion.

The opening word of each beatitude is not an everyday English word, although it is still possible to sneeze in some parts of the world and have someone call out, *Bless you!* The Jerusalem Bible changed the traditional word *blessed* into *happy,* although not to everyone's liking. When *blessed* is used as an adjective it is a translation of the Greek word *makarios.* The Greek *makar* was associated with the life of the immortal gods. So *makarios, blessed,* means sharing in the life, happiness and joy of God. In other words what we have here is another word to describe communion with the very life of God. It is a word to describe transformation, or the more traditional word holiness.

<hr>

Blessed are the poor in spirit, theirs is the kingdom of heaven

Jesus begins with that challenging and radical affirmation. This beatitude is primary and foundational because Jesus is revealing the lie behind the serpent's invitation to Adam and Eve, *Take this fruit and you will be like God, knowing good and evil.* When we appear, in honest and humble poverty, before God we don't need to take anything. All we have to do is receive unconditional love and acceptance. This is a humiliation for the ego; it demands that we acknowledge God's sovereignty, not our own. It addresses the primary human sin: that we want to be God and that is why it is the primary beatitude. What we thought we had to take for ourselves is given freely to the person who has nothing.

The poor, those who have nothing, are least likely to defend the ego. The poor are sacraments of the brokenness I do not wish to own in myself. In recent months I have been in contact with a number of asylum seekers, many of whom have suffered endless rejections, have been stripped of their dignity, and yet I find in them a freedom to speak the truth, and even a joy amidst so much pain. The very poor are indeed icons of that emptiness that all of us need before God. They have nothing to protect, or to prove. Matthew speaks of the poor in spirit, of interior poverty. This is a real challenge for all of us to move from religion in the head, where I can enjoy my status as *one of the saved,* or as *a good Catholic,* to a conversion of heart in which I acknowledge my vulnerability and brokenness. The poor are visual aids of the inner poverty which all of us experience and usually deny. Real prayer, and real encounters with the poor, will challenge our desire to be seen as a spiritual success story; admired by all.

So we see that the beatitudes are not another set of moral rules to help us win favour with God. They are a means of transformation, moving from my ego agenda of success and advancement, to God's agenda. God will push us further and further into life's problems and difficulties; he will not protect us from them. He identifies with the poor, the rejected and the victims of injustice. The beatitudes do not so much tell us what to do; they tell us who God is for us: *loving Father,* and who I am in the eyes of God: *beloved son or daughter.*

Blessed are the meek, for they will inherit the earth

I think that meekness refers to the non-dominative use of power, to that humble embrace of non-violence. Christian service should try to avoid any kind of imposition of Gospel values. Jesus never imposes; he simply invites. The danger is that we associate the words gentleness and meekness with weakness and softness. Suffice to say that meekness means trying to follow God's will rather than our own, and this can demand very real courage because it will set both men and women against the tenor of secular society. Not in an angry, judgmental way, but in a way that opposes unjust systems. The rich and powerful are just as much victims as are the poor. All are worthy of the gentle mercy of God. This beatitude also invites us to a greater gentleness with ourselves as well as others. Francis de Sales said that one of the best exercises in gentleness is to be patient with ourselves and our imperfections.

Blessed are those who mourn, for they will be comforted

I mentioned earlier that we western Catholics tend to live our spiritual lives in our heads. Other traditions are less cerebral. The eastern Syrian fathers, such as Ephrem and Simeon, have a much healthier respect for the body. Ephrem says that we only need two gifts in life: the gift of joy and the gift of tears. In some respects they are two sides of the same coin. They go to the heart of the Paschal Mystery, the great pattern that Jesus leaves us. The only way to live God's dream for the world today is to share its sorrows and to celebrate its joys.

Tears can be tears of sorrow or tears of joy. God seems to have given us the gift of tears as a vital part of our healing. Tears do cleanse and heal. When you look at the lives of the great saints and the mystics, the closer they got to God in prayer the more they wept over their own sins, and the sins of the world. It seems to be the case that there are parts of the heart that can only be touched by human suffering. As we look into our inner lives we may need to shed tears over past wounds. This too is a healing process. Jesus wept tears at the death of his friend Lazarus, and he wept over Jerusalem; a symbol of humanity that would not accept the gift of his unconditional love. Our tears also represent our exile from Eden, from home, from unitive consciousness. There is an important biblical message here. It reaches its supreme form in the lamentations of Jeremiah and the weeping of Rachel for her children. Jesus wept over the city of Jerusalem.

There have been times when the Christian message has been resisted and even violently opposed. This is still true in some parts of the world. In our western satisfied consumer societies it is more a case of indifference and boredom, what the biblical scholar Walter Brueggemann calls *numbness* in the face of the Gospel:

The question facing ministry is whether there is anything that can be said, done or acted in the face of the ideology of hopelessness. [46]

This is a much more challenging task and the Church still has some mourning to do over its exile from people's lives. In biblical spirituality there seems to be no renewal or rebuilding without some genuine grieving over the present and the past, by facing its pain. Mourning is compassion made visible. There is no Resurrection without the Cross. The wounded one is the creator of new life. The wounds eventually become the teachers.

Blessed are those who hunger and thirst for justice; they shall have their fill

---

It is interesting to see the position of this beatitude. Some might think it should be at the beginning since it describes the mission of Jesus. Remember his words in the synagogue: *I have come to bring good news to the poor.* Here it comes after Jesus speaks about the need for humility, meekness and the gift of tears. Why is this? I think it is because, to do justice in the way Jesus wants, we need to have a very humble and non-judgemental heart. We see too many examples of people who work and campaign for social justice, with a lot of anger and a very judgmental attitude to the weaknesses of others. There is little recognition of their need to weep over their own sins, and so the ego remains in charge.

---

[46] Walter Brueggemann *The Prophetic Imagination* (Fortress Press Minneapolis 2001) p 63

When we reflect on the mystery of mercy and forgiveness we are at the heart of the Gospel. You get a real sense of how radical the kingdom is, how amazing the dream of God for all humanity when you realise that neither mercy nor forgiveness can ever be *earned* or *won* from God. They are at the heart of the mystery of grace: totally unearned and abundantly given. This beatitude really does reveal the heart of God. There is no buying or selling here: that is why Jesus violently overturned the tables of the moneychangers in the house of God.

Mercy truly reveals God as one who breaks all the rules of punishment and satisfaction. As we feel the shame of our recurring sinfulness, God just smiles, laughs even, and gives us an accepting embrace, as we see in the parable of the Prodigal Son. Thomas Merton used to say that when we meet God we experience *mercy within mercy, within mercy, within mercy.* God is so humble; he never holds our sins against us. As we receive so should we give. Mercy is not something God *does:* it is who he *is.*

Blessed are the pure in heart, for they will see God

It is very important to see the positioning of this beatitude; it follows the call to build the kingdom by working for a just society. Today, however, I think more is required of us. I don't think we can really pass on God's love to others unless we experience that love in the intimacy of our own hearts. This beatitude reminds us that we are called to the kind of deep union with God which only contemplation can give. We encounter God in our communal prayer, in the liturgy, in our service of others, but especially in the inner depths of our hearts. Spirituality is essentially about seeing. This is the beatitude that allows us to see God, especially in unexpected places.

Service of others alone cannot lead us to the pure-seeing, that this beatitude invites us to experience. We cannot make ourselves contemplatives, but we can create the silence and the reflective pause in our active lives, to give God the opportunity to reveal himself to us in the obscurity of faith. God is always looking into our eyes with love, and the genuine pride of a mother and a father. The question is how often do we look at him? The biblical prophets did not just seek justice; they sought God in the silence of their hearts. They moved from the city; the place of service, to the desert; the place of encounter with the Lord in the humble poverty of their hearts. In the desert our hearts can be transformed by the loving and merciful gaze of God, so that our evangelising activity then becomes truly redemptive. Moments of silent-looking at God are so important in helping us to see what is truly real:

> **If you did nothing but simply sit still each day, silent and still, attentive to your breathing, with your eyes closed or lowered toward the ground, you would be doing yourself a huge favor. You would already be starting the long journey home to God.** [47]

Ultimately spirituality is always teaching us how to see and find our way home.

Blessed are the peacemakers, they will be called children of God

---

This beatitude is one that is assuming greater significance in our times. Christians, thanks to the prophetic leadership of people like Thomas Merton and Martin Luther King, are increasingly being called today to discover the revolutionary significance of non-violence. On the Cross we see that Jesus wants to put an end to any history that simply creates victims. We need to be careful about false patriotism here. It is too facile, and simply dangerous, to divide the world into the good and the bad, because the next step is always the justification, often religiously motivated, of killing my enemy in the name of some kind of righteousness. We have an enormous responsibility to help educate the young to non-violent living. You can be sure that you will not be popular if you do this. You will be classed as dangerous, unpatriotic and subversive, but remember how Jesus tells us that we must be prepared to hate our father, mother, sister, brother etc., for his sake.

Blessed are those who are persecuted for righteousness' sake, for theirs is the kingdom of heaven

---

I was preaching on this once and when I quoted the next words of Jesus, *Blessed are you when people abuse you, and persecute you and speak all kinds of calumny against you on my account,* a priest said to me afterwards that those words apply today to all those working in the Church in the area of child protection. We are still reaping a whirlwind here in the Church and those who work in this field are carrying so much pain on behalf of the perpetrators of child abuse. I think it applies also to anyone who truly embraces the Gospel in this postmodern, deconstructive and cynical world. What we see in these beatitudes is the face of God. If we try to live in this way, our lives will gradually be transformed into an imperfect but very real copy of that face. When we see

---

[47] James Finley *Christian Meditation* (SPCK London 2004) p 26

God's face in the poor and the vulnerable in our ministry, we will also hopefully see God's reflection in the vulnerability of our own hearts.

Living this new spirituality of the beatitudes, of the poor, the gentle, the meek, those who long for justice, leads us into the new grace-filled world that Jesus calls the kingdom of God. It reverses the normal path of history, one that puts down the mighty and raises up the lowly. This is the kingdom proclaimed by Jesus. It centres on, and reveals a very different kind of God from what many expect, even today. In revealing a loving and merciful God who embraced the poor and the lowly, Jesus met fierce opposition which eventually led to his death.

The God of Jesus seems at times to disappoint us. He doesn't solve our problems or provide easy answers. I think we would all prefer a God who gives us clear answers and a clear moral universe. What Jesus does, is draw us into the problems and difficulties of life, and asks us to carry the mystery that leads to transformation. While doing all we can to remove injustice, sometimes all we can do is to suffer with the victims. Some injustices just do not go away. This kind of suffering and frustration at life's unfairness, will either make us bitter or it will transform us. Where it transforms us, compassion is born.

Chapter 7

Male and Female He Created Them

We know that biologically life blossoms forth in the union of the different. I suggest that life within, movement towards the whole, integrity, can also be brought about only through a union of the opposites within us. It is not achieved through a denial of these opposites. [48]

[48] Barbara Fiand *Releasement* (Crossroads NY 1987) p 75

I am a child of Vatican II. I studied for the priesthood in those exciting days after the Council. In those heady years most of my generation, in the naivety of our youthful enthusiasm, were confident that in the battle between liberals and conservatives the liberals would inevitably triumph. Today the picture is rather different and you can read wistful articles asking the question, *whatever happened to Vatican II?* This should not surprise us. The pattern of three steps forward and two steps back, so obvious in the Bible, is no different in our times. It is true for our personal lives and it is true for the Church in general. Mere structural changes, or more consultation, or better planning, even when these occur, will not of themselves make the Gospel come alive in our hearts. The Council warned us about this in stating that all spirituality is summed up in the Paschal Mystery. To live and experience Resurrection there has to be some dying and some suffering.

This spiritual transformation happens when opposites are held in tension: light and dark, sin and grace, strength and weakness, sacred and secular. One of the most powerful signs of our times is the movement and desire to create a better balance and union between, perhaps, the deepest of the opposites, male and female. This cultural movement poses special problems for Christianity, which for so many years has suffered from a predominance of masculine over feminine and a completely male authority structure. Perhaps the current decline of the Church in size and influence is allowing a new and richer unity to emerge. As Thomas Merton reminds us in his poem Hagia Sophia, the *anima* only comes to a man when he is little, poor and without defence, truly humble and stripped of protective masks. Hagia Sophia is *Anima,* Holy Wisdom. In a letter to his friend Victor Hammer, Merton wrote:

The feminine principle in the world is the inexhaustible source of creative realizations of the Father's glory. She is his manifestation in radiant splendor! But she remains unseen, glimpsed only by a few. [49]

The letter to the Ephesians reminds us that the mission of Christ is to reconcile all things. In the Bible, truth is frequently revealed by the outsider, and it is Paul, the great outsider among the apostles, who understands the universal reconciling mission of God in Jesus. The gift of grace undercuts all religious systems of worthiness, of insiders and outsiders, winners and losers. As an outsider, Paul understood this better than anyone in the early days of Christianity, as he makes clear in this passage from Romans in the Peterson translation:

---

[49] Quoted by Robert G Waldron in *Thomas Merton In Search Of His Soul* (Ave Maria Press Ind. 1994) p 110

So where does that leave our proud Jewish claims and counterclaims? Cancelled? Yes, cancelled. What we've learned is this: God does not respond to what we do; we respond to what God does. We've finally figured it out. Our lives get in step with God and others by letting him set the pace, not by proudly or anxiously trying to run the parade. And where does that leave our proud Jewish claim of having a corner on God? Also cancelled. God is the God of outsider non-Jews as well as insider Jews. How could it be otherwise since there is only one God? God sets right all who welcome his action and enter into it, both those who follow our religious systems and those who have never heard of our religion. By shifting the focus from what we do to what God does don't we cancel out all our keeping of the rules and ways God commanded? Not at all. What happens, in fact, is that by putting that entire way of life in its proper place, we confirm it. [50]

God's plan, therefore, is to bring things together not to divide, to unite opposites not to dismiss them. We become transformed by holding together and living in the tension of opposites. So Paul does not dismiss the Law; he reveals its true purpose, as a guardian to protect us until the gift of God's grace reveals our true identity as sons and daughters of God:

But now that faith has come, we are no longer subject to a disciplinarian, for in Christ Jesus you are all children of God through faith. As many of you as were baptized into Christ have clothed yourselves with Christ. There is no longer Jew or Greek, there is no longer slave or free, there is no longer male and female; for all of you are one in Christ Jesus. And if you belong to Christ, then you are Abraham's offspring, heirs according to the promise. [51]

Paul is a very radical thinker and he is struggling to understand and communicate the great mystery of Christ. Our western minds are trained to be logical and rational whereas Paul constantly uses paradox to push us into the great mystery of who Christ is for us. Clearly, even in Paul's time, Jewish and Greek identity did not disappear. There were still slaves and free men, and obviously male and female. What Paul is trying to suggest is that racial, political and even gender differences were not primary. There has to be some kind of union of these opposites, some coming together at a deep level. Technical reason tries to cancel out opposites as contradictory; it is *either/or* thinking. Paradox leads to a wisdom that can allow opposites to reveal a

[50] Romans 3:27-31
[51] Galatians 3:25–29

deeper truth; it is *both/and*. Jesus was a *both/and* teacher; and so is Paul, but for the last thousand years or so western civilisation has been trapped in left brain, *either/or* thinking and analysis, and the right brain, the domain of the feminine has been downgraded if not ignored. Most of the teaching of Jesus is right brain: he uses stories, parables and symbols; he seeks to include those who feel excluded.

In speaking of the male and female Paul is touching on perhaps the deepest human polarity of all. Even today we say that men are from Venus and women from Mars. The challenge of psychological maturity invites us all to grow by way of integration and the spiritual journey calls us to unify the opposites through the challenge of transformation. A healthy masculine always includes an element of the feminine and vice versa. Jung describes a man's feminine dimension as the *anima;* the woman's masculine dimension is the *animus.* This search for wholeness and integration is one of the great spiritual challenges of our times. It places us right at the heart of the relational paradox; we cannot save ourselves, we are essentially limited; what we crave for we often block and deny.

It is commonly accepted among spiritual writers today that for some centuries we have all suffered, both men and women, from a dualism and imbalance which has placed masculine over feminine. Where Paul was so much at home with paradox, *when I am weak then I am strong etc.,* our western minds have long been colonised by dualism as Barbara Fiand points out:

> **For the dualistic mind what is different is seen as contradictory and irreconcilable; what is weak can never be strong; what is dark can never be light; what is bad never good, what is female never male. That much of reality gives itself to us in pairs of polar opposites and needs to be held in consciousness as a polar tension of dynamic energy is unacceptable to the dualistic interpreter of reality. [52]**

In our current culture of deconstructive postmodernism we are beginning to sense a need for a new kind of wholeness. One of the great prophets of postmodernism, Jacques Derrida, who died recently, became preoccupied with religion in the last decade of his life. He knew that religion was impossible without uncertainty. We human beings with our very imperfect minds can never understand or explain the mystery of God. This conclusion is so relevant today as we live in a world in which people daily kill and attack others in the name of God and religious differences. Derrida counters this evil and

---

[52] Barbara Fiand *Releasement* (Crossroad New York 1987) p 56

negativity, not by counselling despair, but by calling for a different kind of belief and truth, one that includes uncertainty and allows us to see the truth in the stranger, the marginalised and the person who is different. This is moving beyond the logic of rationalism to the mystery of wisdom, that knows its limits and its needs.

This search for wisdom, for a more relational truth, for the willingness to live with uncertainty, is one that moves to include right brain thinking, and right brain spirituality. It rejects all elements of fundamentalism and triumphalism. It can live with ambiguity; it is less strident, less judgmental and more compassionate. We are constantly being invited into a mystery which we cannot control:

> **Because our spiritual journey is not a theological exercise, it does not reward us with increasing clarity. Rather it submerges us ever more deeply in mystery.** [53]

Where left-brain thinking argues at the level of ideas, concepts and analysis, the right brain seeks connections, is more personal and relational. Although we can push the gender words too far, I believe that it is accurate to say that the soul is feminine while the spirit is masculine. Soul connects us with our innermost selves, with depth, it is not afraid of mystery. Spirit is what pushes us out in the necessary masculine journey to reach for stars and to create a better world. For too long western spirituality has sought spirit without the necessary soul journey.

Because of the long-standing preponderance of masculine over the feminine there is a great need today to get in touch with our souls, with our inner lives. To say that the soul is feminine, points to a profound spiritual truth; it affects, for example, the way we pray. In giving retreats in different parts of the world I am always struck by the number of times religious people confess distractions in prayer. This is because we have all been taught that prayer equals thinking. So if my thoughts drift off then I cannot be praying. One of the greatest challenges before the Church today is to move the emphasis from our rather exclusive guidance in the moral sphere to include the mystical sphere. As we have seen in earlier chapters, we do not need to feel that God dislikes us and requires a series of good moral actions to increase our worthiness in his eyes. *Being* always comes before *doing; ontology* before *morality.* The feminine gift of receiving, as we see modelled perfectly in Mary, is the foundational act in the spiritual life. In the second half of life we learn that spirituality is more about surrender than control. Men tend to struggle with that

[53] John Kirvan *Raw Faith* (Sorin Books Notre Dame Ind. 2000) p 176

more than women, because we have been taught that the spiritual life was all about effort and achievement.

If God, as we have seen in the Bible, is calling us to a relationship of unitive consciousness and communion, then it leads naturally into a genuine experience of intimacy. Prayer is not something I have to do to win God's favour; prayer is getting in touch with what is truly real. It takes us beyond the agenda of the false self into a deep awareness of who I am in God. We can pray in all sorts of ways, all of them good, but I am speaking about wordless prayer, prayer beyond ideas and concepts, prayer which is simply awareness at the deepest level of soul. It is prayer as presence, shifting the emphasis from me and my needs, to a simple awareness of God. This cannot be put into words but is experienced at a very profound level. We are moving here from meditation to the edges of contemplation.

The Church is being called today to a rediscovery of the Sacred Feminine. We are being called to move beyond the great control and moralising needs, which demand constant and merciless judgement of others, including ourselves. We end up with very small people, going around protecting their small-minded certainties. No wonder so many are turned off religion by its petty righteousness. That little moral ego has to die when we face up to the fact that none of us can be perfect. We are all a mass of contradictions and we cannot afford to take ourselves too seriously. We are called to love ourselves as we are. In fact one of the most significant and important acts in the spiritual life is to accept who I am, warts and all. This is how I am loved and saved by the God of Jesus, not through my perfection but in my imperfections. Here in this experience of what has been rightly called *amazing grace,* the spirituality of compassion is born.

This is moving into the second stage of life, what St Paul in his letters calls mature spirituality, or today we call it transformation. It is powerfully expressed by John Sanford in these words:

> **It becomes clear that the ethic of the kingdom of God is more paradoxical than we have dared let ourselves suppose. The person who becomes a child of the Father is not, after all, going to be the pure human being, but will be one in which a growing knowledge and acceptance of himself – or herself – has developed a unique capacity for love. Not righteousness but love, not following rules but conscious self-acceptance, are the keys to the kingdom of God. [54]**

[54] John Sanford *The Kingdom Within* (Harper San Francisco 1987) p 93

Salvation is brought to us and felt within the limitations of our human experience. We learn to accept we are a mass of contradictions and we are called to live as images of the essential truth of our humanity, that we are at the same time carriers of glory and of weakness. The glory is not of our making; it is received as pure gift and that is why the soul is feminine before God. While Mary is the great model of this kind of receptive faith and love, we also see it exemplified in a masculine form by John, the beloved disciple.

In that dramatic scene at the Last Supper we find Jesus deeply troubled. His message of a relational God who calls us into union and intimacy has met all kinds of resistance from the Scribes and Pharisees. Many ordinary people have also been reluctant to come to the banquet of the kingdom. Now one of his closest friends is about to betray him. This must have been a cause of immense suffering to Jesus. At this point John is described as resting in the *kolpos,* the bosom of Jesus. Peter knows that John seems to have a greater degree of intimacy than the other disciples, so he prompts him to ask Jesus about the identity of his betrayer. The dipping of the morsel was yet another gesture of friendship to his betrayer. But it is the image of John that is so striking. To the modern masculine it appears almost effeminate. I think what is important here is that is only a stage, but a vital stage, in the masculine journey. The journey of John into personal intimacy needs to be complemented by a journey outwards to embrace the world.

The reconciling of masculine and feminine, in a new creative unity, is one of the great spiritual challenges of our times. Women in the west have fought hard for their dignity and rights to be recognised. They are now able to operate in the masculine world of work and employment, in positions of power and responsibility. It could be argued that there is still some way to go for full equality, yet the direction is clear. The problem for women, is that in developing their masculine side, they may forfeit some of the relational values of the true feminine. Men, on the other hand, can get stuck in the soft feminine world. If full consciousness is to be realised, women have to make the journey into the masculine and then back again into the mature feminine. For men the opposite is true. They have to make the journey from shallow masculine into the feminine, but not remain there. They then have to re-engage with the mature masculine.

The integration of the masculine and the feminine will not occur if either gender seeks to dominate the other. A true partnership will acknowledge the need to unite these great gender differences for the sake of humanity. An unbalanced masculine agenda often leads to the misuse of power and reinforces the trend to violence or bullying, and the use of coercion in response both to relational matters, as well as wider problems. We see so many men unable to commit themselves to permanent relationships, leaving single mothers struggling to bring up the children. So many young people today suffer from what is called the *father wound.* This is caused by the absent father. The absence of the mother creates the *mother wound.* In the wider world we see the increasing use of violence, war and force, to effect change. There is an inability to engage in the long haul of building new kinds of relationships. The current situation in Iraq and the Middle East shows the poverty of that kind of response, as violence simply begets more violence. In the Church we see the over-reliance on masculine thinking with its emphasis on logic and reason, its search for certainty, for winners and losers, its moralising attitude. This is often more judgmental than compassionate. We see all power concentrated in the hands of celibate male clergy.

With an all male authority set-up in the Church, it is not surprising that we have put more energy into the managerial and organisational side of the Church than leading people towards transformation. The Church has highly developed its canon law, its liturgical rules and rituals and codes of morality; there has been less emphasis on the mystical journey and social transformation. Too much energy and debate in the Church today is locked into the level of internal Church affairs, rather than the prophetic challenge to read the signs of the times.

On the other hand, in secular society, we see the feminisation of what might be called the domestic, the soft feminine in our culture. So many television programmes deal with makeovers of homes and gardens. For many successful men the only point of life seems to be the task of creating a bigger or more beautiful home. In itself there is nothing wrong with this, but we have to ask, why did Jesus warn against the pull and the attraction of the domestic, of the family. I think this is what he is getting at in these very challenging words:

> **Do not think that I have come to bring peace to the earth; I have not come to bring peace, but a sword. For I have come to set a man against his father, and a daughter against her mother, and a daughter-in-law against her mother-in-law; and one's foes will be members of one's own household.** [55]

---

[55] Matthew 10: 34–36

The sword is one of the great masculine images. True religion always leads us to blood. Transformation cannot really happen without the shedding of blood, the death of the false self, nor can the world begin to be transformed without the agenda of the beatitudes, the commitment to stand alongside the poor and the disadvantaged.

A spirituality of compassion is not about softness, of choosing the comfortable. When we widen the circle of compassion, in the way that the Gospel asks us, we commit ourselves to the masculine task of giving soul to our world. This is a task for mature men and for mature women, and it is interesting again to see that Mary is told that her soul will be pierced by a sword. In the great Magnificat prayer, that Luke brilliantly places on Mary's lips, we see the supreme example of a spirituality that embraces both the personal and the political. In the recent years of renewal, so many religious and lay women have led the struggle for social justice.

A true marriage of male and female strengths and weaknesses recognises that no individual can do it alone, nor any nation, nor any race; certainly not any gender. God has given us the great attraction of masculine and feminine to teach us that, as woman and man combine to create a new human person, men and women are also called to create a new world together. This new consciousness of partnership will help overcome the old patriarchy that placed strength, power and logic above the softening of the relational. The new relational consciousness will have the courage to work for a truly inclusive justice that recognises and fights, with a warrior's sword, for the poor and the excluded. It will work, not to defeat the oppressors, but to try to include them in the building of a more soulful world.

A compassionate spirituality will be built on the need for *The Other.* None of us is complete. None of us is perfect. Instead of seeing the one who is different as a threat or a source of fear, as the old consciousness told us, we can move to a new level of recognition and respect for the truth of *The Other,* the truth that I need in order to grow and mature. Instead of simply conquering rivals or despoiling the planet, in the search for more wealth, a more equal partnership with the feminine will lead to new creativity.

The Church still has some way to go in this whole area. In many ways the Church is trapped in the soft feminine. For too long we have distorted the image of Mary and seen her as the model of the soft virtues of patience, of submission, of not rocking the boat. Men need to integrate the relational gifts of John, the beloved disciple, with the more fiery, warrior gifts of the prophet John the Baptist. The opposite is true: the justice of the Baptist needs to be tempered by the compassionate love of John the beloved. Women need to integrate the motherly warmth and humility of Mary, with the woman who is described, in a wonderfully whole image in the Apocalypse, as adorned with the *masculine* sun with the *feminine* moon at her feet.

One of the unfortunate developments in the renewal of the Church, called for by Vatican II, has been the continued divide between the personal and the political. It is not uncommon in many parishes to find a prayer group and a social justice group. The two rarely seem to come together, yet both need each other for the kind of wholeness I have been arguing for, in this chapter. Perhaps all of us Christians need to engage more with people who are different from ourselves. Those who pray, a more feminine image, need to move out to engage with victims of injustice, a more masculine image. Those who work for justice need to temper their activism with the inner journey of prayer and reflection. The two great spiritual journeys, the journey within, into the feminine, and the journey without, into the masculine, need to be combined as one journey.

We all resist wholeness and yet here lies our true destiny. The world of male patriarchy should not be replaced by a matriarchal world. This would serve neither men nor women. The feminist movement has allowed women the possibility of being taken more seriously than they have in the past, although the Church seems to have a long way to go in this respect. Real change also needs new structures, more circular, less hierarchical. One of the good effects of feminism has been the growth in rediscovering masculine spirituality. This is a great opportunity for both genders to construct a more human environment, a more collaborative style of working, a more non-violent way of life.

A new synthesis of male and female will lead to a newly compassionate spirituality, one that pursues both the inner and the outer journey with equal vigour and creativity. Real change in our Church, and in our world, will not come about if it is imposed from above. It has to grow from within. This is the wisdom of the feminine that the Holy Spirit is breathing into our world today. It is a wisdom that also calls for the masculine energy of engagement with the injustices of our time. Such a holistic spirituality will lead us to a compassionate engagement with our contemporary problems of violence, prejudice, education, health and family values. We may not solve these problems, but if we can be truly compassionate towards our own failings, and therefore the failings of others, we can at least work towards inclusive rather than exclusive solutions. God is the great re-cycler. He is teaching us to find more creative ways of using all our strengths and weaknesses.

Chapter 8

The Cross as the Way Through

We live in a time when there dawns upon us a realisation that the people living on the other side of the mountain are not made up exclusively of red-headed devils responsible for all the evil on this side of the mountain. [56]

[56] Carl Jung

I began this book by looking at the issue of fear as one of the dominant forces shaping our times. The biblical story gradually, and hesitantly at times, reveals a God not to fear but one who invites us into a relationship of love intimacy, as we discover our true identity as beloved of God. The work of God is revealed as the reconciling of opposites. He does this, not by punishing or defeating *The Other,* but by including the rejected and denied parts of our humanity in the great work of reconciliation and redemption. He invites mankind beyond a religion of sacrifice and duty, to one of relationship and participation in the great mystery of life. This reconciling mission includes everything human in the mystery of forgiveness.

As part of his plan he seems to choose certain people who can be visual aids of what he is trying to do for all humanity. Hence the importance of community, as sign and symbol of relationships, characterised by forgiveness and compassion. Christian communities are not idealistic places of perfection and sinlessness. They reflect God's goodness by welcoming differences, leading to a self-acceptance that develops a humble and honest way of life. Community reminds us that we cannot make the spiritual journey alone; there really is no such thing as an autonomous Christian. As we learn to live compassionately with our own defects and weaknesses, we can then reach out to welcome those who are different from us; *The Other.* Christian community is not a gathering of the favoured and the saved, and certainly not the spiritually superior, but a sign of the reconciling of differences that mirrors the plan of God to bring all things together in Christ.

Such a path is truly challenging and the Bible reveals a people struggling with a God who is inclusive, not exclusive, who appears to have a special predilection for the poor and the oppressed, who often uses the outsider as the carrier and revealer of truth. As opposites are reconciled, the true richness of God's plan is made manifest. Nothing is left out, or excluded. As we saw in the last chapter, this process reaches its completion in Christ in whom, as Paul reminds us, *there is neither Jew nor Greek, slave or free person, male or female.* Gradually we see the face of a loving compassionate God who turns history on its head, as he invites his followers into the transforming path of the beatitudes. The normal way of reading history from the top, from the perspective of the winners, is completely reversed. The poor and the wounded become the teachers.

The whole message of Jesus is revealed as welcoming the stranger, forgiving the sinner, the prostitute, the tax collector, the enemy in whatever shape. At the same time of course he is teaching us to accept and forgive the enemy within. This is not easy for the human ego, for even religious people want to be in control, to feel good, to feel superior, even when we are reaching out to the poor and the weak. This is why the great task of the second half of life is to move from control to surrender. This involves the death of the ego and rising to a new life of compassion and serenity, which becomes clear in the later Wisdom Books of the Bible.

How we deal with our fears is becoming one of the primary spiritual questions of the age, as we see the effects of fundamentalism clashing in many parts of the world. Many societies are struggling with differences, with other faiths and multiculturalism, and an influx of refugees and asylum seekers who are often perceived as a threat to a particular culture and way of life. These are not new fears; in fact they are rooted in one of the most pervasive strains of human history: the need to create victims. The victim, once identified, becomes the carrier of all human evil. The next step is to destroy and kill the victim who has thus assumed the role of scapegoat. In the writings of thinkers, such as René Girard and Gil Bailie, this process of victimising and scapegoating is described as sacred violence. [57]

Scapegoating is usually directed at the *outsider,* or the one who is physically or mentally deficient, or the one with a different colour of skin, or a different nation, or a different faith.

The world today is struggling to contain the threat of religiously inspired terrorism. In fact religion, in some form or other, is at the heart of many of our current problems. The present American government is strongly supported by Christian fundamentalists. What seemed an easy military victory in Iraq has degenerated into daily violence. We have witnessed the degradation and torture of prisoners in Abu Ghraib and Guantanamo Bay. Western hostages have been beheaded in barbarous fashion, and those trying to rebuild Iraq are ruthlessly attacked or killed. The Middle East is still trapped in a religiously fuelled conflict. The rise of suicide bombers is linked to religious fanaticism, the most dramatic example of which we witnessed in the attack on the World Trade Center. In Northern Ireland some religious leaders have persistently blocked attempts at reconciliation between rival Christian communities. In England we have recently witnessed a play being withdrawn from public performance in Birmingham because of Sikh protests which turned violent, sparking a debate about freedom of speech and the rights of religious believers not to be insulted. We see bitter struggles between those who argue

[57] For a fuller discussion see G Bailie *Violence Unveiled:* Humanity at the Crossroads (Crossroad NY 1995) and R Girard *Violence and the Sacred* (John Hopkins UP Baltimore, 1977).

for the right to life and their opponents. We witness the stigmatisation of those suffering from HIV-AIDS. Whatever we say about it, religion is embedded in so many of the world's problems and its influence often seems to fuel violent solutions.

What the Hebrew and Christian scriptures reveal is that human beings almost instinctively wish to push evil onto someone else, or onto another nation. Someone else is always to blame; it is never me. In the Genesis story of the Fall we see Adam blaming Eve, and Eve blaming the serpent. Genesis also tells the story of Cain murdering his brother out of envious revenge, thus setting in train the whole pattern of human history: *the identifying and the killing of the victim.* What seems to characterise evil is its claim to certainty. There is no room for doubt or complexity. Countries are accused of being the axes of evil, a refinement of the old evil empire, so enemies hit back by calling the West, *the great Satan.* The evil is always *over there,* always without, never within.

Genuine spirituality, real faith in other words, is just the opposite. Real faith is capable of carrying the mystery of what it means to be human. Being human involves the capacity to carry a fair amount of anxiety. Despite all our efforts at discernment, we can never truly be sure that we are doing the will of God. Real faith leads us into a certain amount of complexity. This is where transformation can begin to happen, when we learn to carry the mystery of human complexity and paradox. This is a crucial spiritual insight. If it is not faced up to and admitted, then what inevitably happens is that evil is projected onto someone else. It might be the person I don't like, it might be the stranger, it might be another race or faith, or another gender. This also happens within families and within communities.

In the unfolding of the biblical story, the scapegoating and blaming found in Adam and Cain is almost sacralised in an amazing passage in Deuteronomy, as the people are being guided into the Promised Land:

Make no covenant with them and show them no mercy. Then the anger of the Lord would be kindled against you, and he would destroy you quickly. But this is how you must deal with them: break down their altars, smash their pillars, hew down their sacred poles, and burn their idols with fire.

The next sentence goes on, to justify and excuse all this behaviour and is the classic explanation for what Bailie and Girard call sacred violence:

For you are a people holy to the LORD your God; the Lord your God has chosen you out of all the peoples on earth to be his people, his treasured possession. [58]

This passage uncovers one of the central problems of all religion and religious experience, and it is one that is rarely addressed or acknowledged. What we see recorded honestly in the Bible is the developing religious consciousness of a people. I think it is evident that God would not sanction or propose this kind of violence. At times the chosen people gloried in their election by God, and it was a short step from there to feeling superior to other nations. Such a feeling of superiority, especially as they felt it was backed by God, allows them to deal with different races and peoples by suppressing them violently. It is not uncommon for religious experience to lead initially to inflation. If you are told you are special in the eyes of God, the ego quickly takes over and presumes superiority over others. The most dangerous form of scapegoating is to do it for religious reasons, in the name of God. That is sacred violence, and it describes much of the religious history of mankind.

Healthy religion and spirituality eventually leads to the central demand for some kind of conversion, metanoia, or transformation. Unless that happens we remain stuck in the first part of life's journey and continue repeating it. Religion then becomes a place to hide from God, by substituting behaviour and ritual instead of transformation. We see this classically illustrated by Jesus in his parable of the Pharisee and the Publican. We see it again in the parable of the prodigal son, when the law-abiding brother is unable to forgive. We see it in the parable of the Good Samaritan, when the religious leaders and temple officials pass by the man in need.

Too much religion leaves us at what I called, in the fifth chapter, the second level of *Our Story*. We take pride, a justifiable pride, in our religion, our nation and our patriotism, but we do it in a way that makes us feel superior to others. Politicians know that there is no better way to unite a country than to declare a common enemy.

Much of what I am saying in this chapter has been learned from the work of contemporary prophets like Richard Rohr and René Girard. Rohr is surely correct when he says that the great challenge to our spirituality is how to deal with evil without becoming evil, how to deal with hate without becoming hateful. All religions agree that evil has to be resisted and overcome, but the central spiritual question is, *how?* Without some sort of transformation we will

---

[58] Deuteronomy 7:1–7

not get to this point. At the beginning of the modern world, the period known as the Enlightenment, it was thought that education would do this. Education would be the answer to all the worlds' evils, which it was felt, were based on ignorance. Yet one of the most educated of nations allowed itself to be overcome by the scapegoating myths of fascism. Some very educated people can be caught up in the mechanism of scapegoating. Currently in the UK we see tabloid newspapers stirring up prejudice against asylum seekers and refugees. Someone else must carry our pain.

All human history has struggled with the problem of how to deal with evil. As long as we keep projecting it onto others we will be living inside what has been called *the myth of redemptive violence:* the belief that if somebody hits me, and if I hit them back, preferably even harder, then some kind of redemption has taken place. This myth of redemptive violence is extremely difficult to refute, because in the short term it appears to work. A spirituality that is real, and genuinely engaged with the world, needs to address this issue. One of the dangers of the recent revival in spirituality is to see it as a kind of personal life-style choice, like a new diet or keep-fit exercise. In healthy spirituality the personal has to be married to the political, the feminine with the masculine, the inner with the outer. [59] Thomas Merton makes this point with his usual clarity:

What is wanted now is therefore not simply the Christian who takes an inner complacency in the words and example of Christ, but who seeks to follow Christ perfectly, not only in his own personal life, not only in prayer and penance, but also in his political commitments and in all his social responsibilities. [60]

Christians today are learning to respect all faiths but we do claim that Jesus Christ is the Saviour of the world. I think there is something quite radical about the mystery of Jesus that is now beginning to emerge in our world today. Mankind seems to have reached a stage in consciousness when we can begin to see how revolutionary the message of Jesus really is. This is not a Church thing, because there are many practising Christians still locked into the myth of redemptive violence and scapegoating, whereas there are some outside the Christian Church who understand what is at stake and are living it. In the end it all seems to come down to transformation.

Christian faith and spirituality has always proclaimed that the rejection, suffering, death and the resurrection of Jesus is the great symbol, and the key to all human history. At the same time the suffering and death of Jesus reveals

---

[59] This theme is explored more fully in *Within & Without* (Don Bosco Publications 2002)
[60] Thomas Merton *Peace in the Post-Christian Era* (Orbis Books Maryknoll NY 2004) p 131

what God is doing in our souls. This pattern, what we call the Paschal Mystery, is the great icon and symbol of our personal and collective histories. The mystery of the Cross is the way to understand everything, but again it doesn't mean that everyone who understands it is necessarily living it. It seems that we Christians are given the privilege to name the mystery. The grace and wisdom of God is active in many who may not be aware of it. But there is no doubt that all the themes of the Bible come to a head and a resolution in the rejection, suffering and death of Jesus.

This is made evident in a telling passage in John's Gospel:

> **Now is the judgment of this world; now the ruler of this world will be driven out. And I, when I am lifted up from the earth, will draw all people to myself.**[61]

John sees the death of Jesus on the Cross as the great overcoming of the lie, spread by the prince of this world, the accuser, the one who puts forward the false meaning of history: the need to create victims. In contrast and through the experience of rejection and suffering, Jesus draws all people to the true meaning of history; the story of God's grace and his unconditional love. We are drawn into this mystery when we realise that evil is not over there, but that I am part of it.

There are many biblical images that pre-figure this mystery, but one of the most powerful is the figure of the scapegoat. The scapegoat is the rejected victim, the one who bears the burden, the one who carries the mystery. Another powerful image is the Passover Lamb, which in many ways has lost its power to shock. The people were asked to take the lamb into their house for four days and then kill it. The family will have grown to love the lamb, so it is a powerful symbol of the death of innocence, the death of a loved one. The scapegoat is the rejected victim and the lamb is the innocent victim. In Zechariah, chapter 12, we have the theme of mourning over the one they have pierced. This is grief work: the need to enter into pain and shed our tears, something that men traditionally struggle with. This mystery of transformation seems to require some form of looking. We find this theme also in the advice from Moses to look upon the serpent, and receive healing; the very serpent which has wounded them. The figure of the Suffering Servant is another powerful way of revealing the scapegoat mechanism. All these images reach their fulfilment in Jesus, the innocent victim who dies on the Cross with no cry for vengeance; the only cry is a plea to his Father for forgiveness.

---

[61] John 12:31–32

In the story of our history we found a way of dealing with evil, other than by forgiveness. We opted instead for some kind of system that demanded someone be tortured, punished or sacrificed. In the great reversals of the scriptures the greatest one is that God does not want anyone to be sacrificed. God does not want or require anyone's blood, for us to become acceptable to him. In fact the opposite is true. In the mystery of the Cross, God sheds his blood for us. It was the medieval theologian, Duns Scotus, who said that Jesus did not have to die to pay any kind of ransom for our sins; he died to reveal the compassionate and forgiving heart of God. On the Cross he reveals the true meaning of history. He is telling us to stop creating victims. In the mystery of being lifted up he asks us to keep looking at this mystery of forgiveness. He doesn't just tell us about it. He acts it out before our eyes, to reveal that it is possible to live beyond and outside of the lie embedded in the false story of history, one that requires victims and scapegoats.

In the mystery of the Cross we see God not just pleading with us to stop creating victims; he becomes the victim. The true story of human history is now fully revealed: God is the victim of human history. Above all he is the forgiving victim, who always sees our true selves. When we suffer unjustly we usually search for someone to blame, someone to punish, someone to kill. With Jesus the opposite happens:

> **Then Jesus said, 'Father, forgive them; for they do not know what they are doing.'** [62]

In these amazing words Jesus unmasks the false story of history as ignorant killing, the process of pushing my pain onto someone else and punishing them for it. Jesus has already predicted that the stone the builders rejected becomes the cornerstone. He himself is rejected by both religious and political leaders; he is abandoned by his friends and followers, denied by Peter, his chosen leader, and yet offers total forgiveness. The wounded one becomes the gift-giver, the bringer of new life. The part of me that I want to deny and reject becomes the means of new life. So instead of a God to be afraid of, one who demands constant sacrifice, we finally see revealed in Jesus a God who suffers with us. In suffering with us he does not look for anyone else to blame or anyone else to punish. What he invites us to is a spirituality of compassion, of acceptance and of wisdom. As he dies he hands over the gift of the Spirit. What happens at Pentecost in Luke, happens at Calvary in John.

A new kind of power is now released into the world. A truly transformative power that reverses the dominative pattern which the world worships in favour

---

[62] Luke 23:34

of the power of the poor person, the powerless one, the rejected one, the one who knows they are wounded. Here again we meet the death of the ego, the death of our presumed innocence and superiority. This kind of power moves to inclusive, rather than exclusive, solutions. Ultimately, when confronted with the reality of evil it refuses to push it onto the other person or the other nation, or the enemy in whatever form. The only solution available is to accept that I am part of the problem. Without that acknowledgement nothing will ever change in a truly transformative way.

It has to lead to transformation, to the revealing of new identity, and in so many ways the world resists this kind of transformation, as John says in the prologue, before he even begins the Gospel of Good News:

He was in the world, and the world came into being through him; yet the world did not know him. He came to what was his own, and his own people did not accept him. But to all who received him, who believed in his name, he gave power to become children of God. [63]

The identity that Adam and Eve wanted to grab for themselves, so they could become like God, is now freely given: the power to become children of God.

What exactly is this *power* that John speaks of? As Richard Rohr says the Cross is about knowing how to fight and resist evil without becoming a casualty yourself. It is an attempt to move beyond *win/lose* solutions and trying to create a *win/win* scenario. It is a refusal to hate and humiliate *The Other* because that would only perpetuate the violence. It is trying to move beyond the scenario of revenge, which we see on our news bulletins, in places like the Middle East, in Northern Ireland, in Bosnia and in Iraq.

We cannot be naïve about evil. The Church struggled to respond to this problem with the theory of a just war which can be fought in certain circumstances. But weapons today are so destructive that we find great leaders such as Pope John Paul II, the Dalai Lama, and Nelson Mandela, calling for new and more creative solutions. René Girard is not alone in saying that there is a new consciousness in our world, inspired by figures such as Gandhi and Martin Luther King. While the old story of scapegoating and attacking others goes on, there are increasing numbers of people who are telling their politicians that they need to find non-violent solutions to the world's problems. The demonstrations that ended the Vietnam War in the 1960s were echoed before the recent Iraq war.

---

[63] John 1:9–12

What the Cross reveals is that the transforming power of God's love and grace always works from within. It rejects any form of coercion or violence. Even the Bible shows how hard it is for human beings not to project violence onto God. All the great images of suffering-love however, that have been present in human consciousness in the unfolding of the biblical story, become clear and compelling in the figure of Jesus. Here we see a different kind of God, revealed not in almighty power, but in weakness, in vulnerability and in suffering. The rejected one, the outsider, the scapegoat, the innocent lamb is revealed as the face of God:

> **The upshot of this is that God can never be recognised as one of the persecutors. God is emphatically denied any involvement with violent actions. Even the Resurrection must be read as his declaration of his absolute non-involvement with violent death much less with the retribution which one would expect to follow the massacre of his Son. [64]**

If dealing with our fears is one of the great spiritual challenges of today, we see that Jesus is even able to transform the power of evil, not by fighting or ignoring the evil, but by transforming it into forgiveness by suffering it. Such transforming love is even able to overcome death, perhaps our greatest fear. In the power of the resurrection, the rejected one, the dead person, becomes the new life-giver. The answer to the postmodern denial of meaning is the Paschal Mystery, which proclaims that there is nothing that God's power cannot transform.

---

[64] Michael Kirvan *Discovering Girard* (Darton Longman & Todd London 2004) p 83

Chapter 9

A Passion for Life

If people were asked after reading through the Gospels to find one word for the kind of person Jesus was many would choose compassionate. His compassionate heart seemed to inform his life. 'And Jesus, seeing the crowds, was moved with compassion.' [65]

[65] Daniel O'Leary *Passion for the Possible* (The Columba Press Dublin 2000) p 213

One of the Syrian fathers, St Ephrem, said that we really only need two gifts in life: the gift of laughter and the gift of tears. These gifts allow us to engage fully in life, to feel its pain, to suffer with those who suffer, but at the same time to rejoice with those who rejoice, and know laughter as a gift of God. By and large Christians are noted for their concern for others, but it is often wrapped up in a quality of earnestness that is more off-putting than attractive. Nietzche once said that he would take Christianity more seriously if Christians actually looked redeemed. We only have one life and it has to be taken seriously, but at the same time we should not take ourselves too seriously. Not being able to laugh at ourselves usually indicates a lack of awareness of the personal shadow. The other side of the passion and death of Jesus is the Father's raising of Jesus to a new and risen life, which is promised to all of his followers. He shows us that he has come into this world, not to avoid life, but to engage fully with it in all its dimensions.

Much has been said in recent years of the need to develop a holistic spirituality. A truly compassionate and relational spirituality connects with all aspects of life. All of us have been created by, in and for love; this is the great mystery that enfolds all our lives. It leads us to take part in the great dance of life, not to sit on the sidelines protecting our moral purity. In some books of the Bible, holiness was often presented in terms of separation. By the time of Jesus, the different courtyards of the temple simply highlighted these divisions. Jesus went out of his way to break down all these false barriers, between who was worthy and not worthy in the sight of God. He spoke of the unconditional love of God, which removes all notions of worthiness. At the heart of the good news is the gift of grace, which moves us into a totally new way of life, beyond the kind of calculations we capitalist-minded westerners take for granted. Dorothy Day clearly understood this when she remarked that once you read and understand the Gospel, you can no longer make distinctions between the worthy and the unworthy poor. As Jesus died on Calvary the veil of the temple was torn in two, signifying the end of holiness-as-separation. The coming of the Holy Spirit to all the gathered nations at Pentecost was the great sign that everyone has access to God.

The Cross of Jesus reminds us that one of the greatest challenges in life is how we deal with our pain and with evil. We cannot avoid this issue. If we do try to avoid it, we simply project our pain onto someone else. If instead of this projection we learn to hold it and let it teach us, it will inevitably lead to transformation. The Paschal Mystery leads us through pain into a very deep joy and happiness. This is not a simple linear process. There will be times when our lives reflect the Cross and there will be times when it will reflect the joy of the resurrection. More often than not we may experience both at the same time. The passion of Jesus invites us into a compassionate way of life, engaged, loving, joyful and vulnerable.

We have commented in previous chapters how religion has re-emerged as a force in the contemporary world much to the consternation of the great sceptics of the Enlightenment. We have used the words of Chief Rabbi Jonathon Sacks, observing that religion is not the opium of the people: it is the fire. Fire can be dangerous and in the last chapter I tried to examine how so much of religion gets distorted into scapegoating others and offloading the pain and imperfections of life onto the vulnerable stranger, or the distant foreigner, or the person we don't like. This is one of the central spiritual challenges of our time: to discover the transforming spiritual power of a religious passion for life that is centred on love and not on hate, that can accept and live with weakness rather than strength, that lives in honest humility rather than arrogant superiority.

That is why Jesus leads his followers into the transforming path of the beatitudes, where a very different form of power is experienced. The transforming power of the kingdom of God embraces the poor and the meek. It invites us to hunger and thirst, Eucharistic terms for justice. It leads us to shed our tears as we mourn with those who mourn. It calls us to rejoice and be glad when our private little egos are diminished by rejection and suffering. Once again we meet the great reversals of the Gospel. Happiness and joy according to the beatitudes are found in the very opposite of what the world presents as happiness.

This emphatically does not mean that we Christians are anti-life, or even anti-pleasure. In fact the opposite is true. The comedian, Spike Milligan, once said that he would love to read the Gospels and turn over a page to find the phrase, and *Jesus laughed heartily.* Sadly we don't find it, but I am sure that Jesus smiled and laughed a lot. In *The Adolescent,* one of Dostoevsky's characters comments that if you want to glimpse inside a human soul, the best way is to observe a person laugh. He equated goodness with laughing well. Daniel O'Leary situates this gift of laughter in the very act of creation:

It is believed that a deep murmur of laughter was the most profound background to the creation of the world, and that God still wears a constant beatific smile when contemplating

the world, even with all its misfortunes and horrific self-destruction. [66]

At the time when I was Provincial of the British province of the Salesians of Don Bosco, I made a number of visits to Liberia in West Africa. The country was in the grip of a brutal civil war. Many children had been orphaned, or exploited as boy soldiers, young girls used as prostitutes. Yet I experienced genuine joy and happiness on the faces of many of those suffering people. One of the most powerful symbols of the Resurrection for me occurred on a visit to a convent. The whole building had been destroyed by rebel rocket attacks. The Sisters had rebuilt the convent. On the altar in the chapel they had fashioned candlesticks out of the shells of the rockets which had been fired as weapons of destruction. Now they were symbols of prayer! Joy and optimism are clear signs of the kingdom. Laughter, joy and optimism are rooted in the playfulness of God.

At the same time it seems that some kind of suffering is almost necessary for us to walk the journey of the Paschal Mystery. Much as we would like it to be different, a passionate commitment to life has to experience some kind of defeat, some loss, the death of the ego. All of us resist this as we cling onto our false and manufactured selves. The apostles clearly resisted all of Jesus' predictions of his passion and death. Unless this *death* occurs in us we will never begin the second journey of life. We will continue to repeat the first half of life, as we build up our ego. It doesn't matter whether it is a liberal ego or a conservative ego, or a priestly ego or a spiritual ego. All the great myths and literature of the male spiritual ego include some great moment of defeat, failure or rejection. This is less dramatic in women's stories because they have experienced many smaller defeats and put-downs in life.

Once the ego has suffered and failed, a new self emerges. This too can be dangerous. This was the problem with the spirituality of perfection. Measuring progress, assessing one's holiness and sanctity can be yet another ego trip; it is full of self-regard. So Jesus warns us about the danger of sweeping the devil out of the house, only to find seven more devils replacing him. Conversion or *metanoia* is never something we can control. It has to be surrendered to. This is perhaps the biggest defeat for the ego. We cannot make ourselves holy, we are not God. My life is not about me, I am about life. This is why prayer is so crucial. There is no better way of shifting the emphasis of my life from me to God. This process of transformation is not spectacular, but ordinary, and it is long-term. Transforming moments are hardly ever

[66] Daniel O'Leary *Travelling Light* (The Columba Press Dublin 2001) p 76

dramatic. They are certainly almost always slow and painful. Jesus reminds us that the seed grows in the ground at night, as the farmer sleeps.

The spirituality of compassion is a spirituality not of perfection but imperfection. It consists in holding the opposites together and letting them transform us. The reconciling mission of Jesus is to unite all things, to bring everything together under God, to unite heaven and earth, light and dark, male and female, above and below, suffering and joy. Ultimately all of this reaches its climax at the heart of the Paschal Mystery, the overcoming of death in the Resurrection of Jesus. This is the only pattern for the spiritual life. We never get it all together. Like the biblical figures we take *three steps forward and two steps back.*

It leads us to the humble recognition that we are sinners, that we can never get it right and perfect, and at the same time the realisation that our earthly bodies also carry the mystery of glory. Living in the uncertainty of this kind of faith leads us to realise that original blessing is prior to and more foundational than original sin. This tension between original sin, which is constantly telling us that we are unworthy, and original blessing which says we are fully worthy, as a result of the free gift of grace, is at the heart of the spiritual struggle:

It is hard for us to take God at his word when he says that it is his delight to dwell in the souls of men.

Some souls, we think, might delight him. Those souls where you would expect to find God, where by our standards we judge God might be comfortable. We could understand that.

But it is not just 'some' souls. It is all souls. At all times. No exceptions. His word is good. None of us is left out. None of us. [67]

It is not really a question of us seeking God. He has already found us and delights to be with us. Even though we may not be comfortable with ourselves, he is already comfortable with us. We might give up on ourselves, or on others, but he will never give up on us. This experience is primary and foundational to the spiritual life. What we see revealed in the Bible is the faithful covenant love of God which is described best as *hesed,* which means mercy. As we have been reminded by Thomas Merton, when we meet God we meet mercy *within mercy, within mercy, within mercy.*

The need today is to bring our flesh and blood back into our spirituality. For all kinds of complex reasons in our Christian history we looked on God as unchanging, almighty, detached and largely passionless. The further distortion

---

[67] John Kirvan *Raw Faith* (Sorin Books Notre Dame Ind 2000) p 110

of dualism led to the promotion of spirit at the expense of soul and body. All human passion had to be eliminated from the spiritual life. The theologian, St John Climacus, even suggested that God could not really be the creator of human passions! Purity of heart was understood as a passionless kind of life. The great Christian virtue was detachment.

This was a terrible distortion of the life of Jesus and really a denial of the Incarnation, the Word becoming flesh. In Jesus we don't see a model of detachment. What we see is a deep and vulnerable attachment from a man who is so in love with life and with his friends. He welcomes the stranger, heals the sick, touches the leper, reaches out to the excluded, such as women and children, who even calls for love of enemies, and who was so in love with his friends that he gave up his very life for them. The life of this passionate man was truly and fully human. He embraced all our experiences and emotions. His loving heart and soul opened him up to vulnerability.

One of the most profound and astonishing scenes in the Gospel story is the incident with Thomas in the upper room, when the risen Jesus points to his wounds. I think we would expect the risen body to be perfect and free of wounds and signs of suffering. But Jesus seems almost proud to display his woundedness to us. Once again we see the great reversal at work. Jesus wants us to understand that the rejected one is the one who brings salvation. The wounded one is the gift-giver. The scapegoat has absorbed all the evil and is able to reveal the lie at the heart of all violence. The power that comes from woundedness is one of the great paradoxes of the spiritual life, a point made tellingly by John O'Donohue:

In every life there is some wound that continues to weep secretly, even after years of attempted healing. Where woundedness can be refined into beauty a wonderful transfiguration takes place. For instance compassion is one of the most beautiful presences one can bring to the world and most compassion is born from one's own woundedness. When you have felt deep emotional pain and hurt, you are able to imagine what the pain of the other is like; their suffering touches you. This is the most decisive and vital threshold in human experience and behaviour. The greatest evil and destruction arises when people are unable to feel compassion. [68]

True compassion cannot exist without vulnerability and risk. God took the greatest risk of all in the act of creation, the giving of freedom to humanity to

[68] John O' Donohue *Divine Beauty* (Bantam Press 2000) p 181

accept or reject the divine plan. The cruellest moment of rejection on Calvary is transformed into the great moment of redemption and forgiveness of sin.

Another paradox we are experiencing today is witnessing the Church going through a time of diminishment. Here too we can see the Paschal Mystery at work. A new kind of Church is beginning to emerge from the current crisis. The Church in which I was nurtured in my youth would speak of the foreign missions and we thought of valiant priests and religious, very little lay involvement of any kind, going out to convert pagans in distant parts of the world. The Church at home was much more concerned with ministering to the faithful. We had our own Catholic sub-culture of schools, parishes and various Catholic organisations. Vatican II opened up our defensive world to reach out to other Christian Churches. Today increased mobility is creating our multicultural and multi-faith societies. This brings new opportunities and new dangers, but it has certainly widened our horizons. Healthy religion can make an enormous contribution here. The secular postmodern world is still suspicious of religion and, with some evidence, sees religious passion at the heart of so much of the conflict in our world. One of the most hopeful signs of the times is the growing recognition across so many nations of the need to translate non-violent theory into practice.

In recent years the Catholic Church has been rocked by the scandal of sexual abuse and attempted cover-up by some bishops and Church authorities. The shadow side of a spirituality of perfection is the denial of sin and weakness. The reconciling mission of Jesus leads us to see that even here, in the midst of all this evil and pain, something new can grow. In a very real sense a certain understanding of the Church has had to die: a view of the Church built on clerical power and privilege. The lack of vocations, the ageing of the clergy, the closing and amalgamating of parishes in the western world, is also leading to a humbler and more collaborative ministry. Maybe the Holy Spirit is leading us through this period of diminishment, this time of decline, this time of purification, to a new, a more transformed ministry. This is the Paschal Mystery of the Church. A new and purified Church can take its part in working alongside other faiths, and those of no faith, in building a world of peace with real justice, especially for the poorest.

Since Vatican II we have become more aware of the kingdom of God as well as the Church. We are more conscious of the need to reach out in a ministry of befriending, rather than converting. Our compassion is moving beyond the second level of *Our Catholic Story,* to embrace and celebrate God's wonderful and all-embracing passionate love for creation and for all people on the planet, The Human Story. To do this we have to be seen as people who love and reverence all aspects of life; people who serve the poor and the marginalised: people whose lives indicate a very deep level of joy and happiness. Recently I have been engaged in taking small groups of asylum seekers into Catholic High Schools. I do this because I believe that the best way to break down prejudice is to meet *the stranger, the foreigner* and to see our common humanity. The insight of Levinas, that biblical truth is *The Other,* is so vital for the future of our planet.

I also think that the recovery of friendship, both personal and political, brings warmth and colour to this insight. I have tried to present the story of Jesus as the one who breaks down all barriers and reconciles all things. He does this by living a *both/and* spirituality rather than *either/or.* He always includes rather than excludes. He integrates all the opposites and holds them in creative tension. This reaches its climax on the Cross, when hanging between heaven and earth, between the good and the bad thief; he draws all things to himself. In his risen body he offers nothing but forgiveness to his disciples who had abandoned him. He makes these wounded men, these failures, into the founders of the Church. In giving power to those who have experienced powerlessness, he reveals a new kind of non-dominative power, a power that brings about transformation from within, rather than change from without. He also gives them a new commandment: to love in the same compassionate way that he has loved.

From the very beginning of the biblical story we see God choosing images of what he is trying to do in the whole world. In the Church we are called to be images of transformation, capable of bearing the mystery of sin and glory that is a human life. Today we are rediscovering the spiritual journey in all its mystery. We are moving from having all the answers given to us on a plate, in our books and our catechisms, to a more biblical understanding of faith that leads us out into uncertainty and calls for trust. We are moving from the spirituality of perfection to the spirituality of imperfection. We recognise our weaknesses and failures as the wounds to the ego that become the real gold of our lives. We are moving from observing the letter of the law, with all its rigidity, to the spirit of wisdom, born in humble failure and transformation. We are moving from detachment that keeps our souls safely locked up, to genuine attachment that opens us to vulnerability and passion. In friendship we are discovering the face of God in our neighbour, defined in the widest possible way.

Compassion is the face of our neighbour; compassion and mercy is the face of God. To live with compassion means to learn how to cry and how to laugh with mankind and let that tension open us up to transformation, which is what we used to call holiness. It means living with limitation and poverty, entering life's mystery with vulnerable trust and faith, celebrating its beauty and mourning, its sorrow. We will never get it all together, but we will learn to look at what is human and what is real with immense compassion. We are called to a ministry of friendship.